A
FATHER'S BOOK

O F   T H E
S P I R I T

Also by William Alexander

A MAN'S BOOK OF THE SPIRIT

A

FATHER'S BOOK

O F   T H E
S P I R I T

Daily Meditations

WILLIAM ALEXANDER

AVON BOOKS NEW YORK

A FATHER'S BOOK OF THE SPIRIT is an original publication of
Avon Books. This work has never before appeared in book form.

AVON BOOKS
A division of
The Hearst Corporation
1350 Avenue of the Americas
New York, New York 10019

Copyright © 1997 by William M. Alexander, Jr.
Interior design by Kellan Peck
Published by arrangement with the author
Visit our website at http://AvonBooks.com
ISBN: 0-380-78632-X

Library of Congress Cataloging in Publication Data:

Alexander, Bill.
    A father's book of the spirit / William Alexander.
        p.   cm.
    1. Men—Prayer-books and devotions—English.
    2. Devotional calenders. I. Title.
    BL625.25.A54   1997   97-3900
    291.4'32'0851—dc21   CIP

First Avon Books Trade Printing: June 1997

AVON TRADEMARK REG. U.S. PAT. OFF. AND IN OTHER COUNTRIES, MARCA
REGISTRADA, HECHO EN U.S.A.

Printed in the U.S.A.

QPM   10 9 8 7 6 5 4 3 2 1

*This book is dedicated with love and gratitude
to my dad,
William M. Alexander
1912–1996*

Acknowledgments

Thank you to Carlton Cole, Mark Gero, Lenny Holzer, Sam Keen, John Daido Loori, Hugh O'Haire, and my brother Philip, fathers all.

Thanks to Kamala, Gia, David, Ed, John, Elizabeth, and Willie, the children who surround my heart and enliven it with their own.

For Mom, who cared for Dad in his darkest hours and brought joy and purpose to all the rest.

And my deepest and fondest gratitude to my wife, Pauline, without whom all the rest of it—family, work, and the ordinary stuff of my life—would have no luster, no sparkle, no passion.

My father died only a month before I finished this book. I had written it with him in mind, and his death only made him more present. Dad taught me two very important lessons. One, he taught explicitly. He told me, when I was twelve, never to stop learning. I have done my best to honor that one. The second thing he taught me, he taught with his entire life. He taught me the importance of listening. As the father of two, born twenty-five years apart, and the stepfather of five, I am grateful for that teaching and admit that I have not honored it as well, certainly, as Dad did.

In this book you will find many different types of entries. Some of them are typical of the genre, some are decidedly atypical. They are all dedicated to the propositions of learning and listening, and in that, at least, my father's legacy is preserved.

There are some pages in this book that are harsh, while others are comforting and others yet are damned silly. There are days with specific suggestions and days with prayers and vows. This is a secular book. If there is a religious bias here, it is an Eastern one, and any political bias is on the liberal side. In my own life, I have seen the role of fathering change so dramatically that dogma is more than usually troublesome. I was a terrible father the first time out and am grateful that my daughter and I have begun a long healing process. I am doing a good job now, twenty-five years later, but that reflects not only a change in me but a change in the social expectations to which I respond.

Zen Master Robert Aitken writes of the two worlds: of nurturance and of exploitation. We live in the world of exploitation. If you have any doubts, just look around you. It is the job of the father to move himself and his children into the world of nurturance. The father who insists on his place at the head of the table, "the head of the family," autocratic and unemotional, is living in the world of exploitation. The father who learns to listen to his unique children and to act in their sole best interest is living in the world of nurturance. It is my hope to see more and more fathers inhabit that world.

A
FATHER'S BOOK
O F   T H E
S P I R I T

Whoever teaches his son
teaches not only his son
but also his son's son—
and so on until
the end of generations.
THE TALMUD

There is a child inside all of us—that child is all future generations.

—THICH NHAT HANH

The father carries the child. Every child of every subsequent generation lives with us in our daily lives. The simple decisions we make can either protect the child or expose the child to the ways of harm. We must make no mistake. These children are with us *today*, in this very moment. They form a vast crowd, stretching to the horizon, mute and powerless. As we fathers turn aside from the warrior role and turn to caretaking, we learn to look closely at what we do without thought and see the effect on this great crowd.

What do we think we need today that will steal from all future generations?

If we justify war, it is because all peoples always justify the traits of which they find themselves possessed, not because war will bear an objective examination of its merits.

—RUTH BENEDICT

Can we, as fathers, put out the light of war within us? We will not end war, no matter how hard we wish to, by making war upon it. My "inner warrior" is long past due in the grave. My son and daughter do not need to study war, not from me. If I am not at war, perhaps they will not see war, within or without.

Today is the end of war.

You will find something more in woods than in books. Trees and stones will teach you that which you can never learn from masters.

—Saint Bernard

Our children learn not only what we teach, but how we learn. This second is subtle and fragile. While they are watching us, they are learning our learning. We need to know that we are always learning. Our learning did not end when we finished school, even if we never studied another thing. It is not necessary to intend to learn. We learn. The mind is filled with the images of our places of worship, the words of the places of learning, and the teachings of our masters. Just as we did not stop learning, we never stopped going to school, to temple, or to the masters' room. Our children know this far better than we do. We must examine our learning. What is it? Where does it take place? What do the children learn?

Today I will look deeply at my learning.

The Whiskey on your breath
Could make a small boy dizzy.
—THEODORE ROETHKE

The sorrow and hope of the child holding on to the flawed and distant father can teach our hearts our own deep sorrow. I read these lines and remember thinking, as a child, that my father smelled of corn on dark Michigan evenings, when his eyes were red and his temper up. I read them also and wonder about my daughter in the too few early years of hers we spent together, when, like Dad, I smelled of ethanol's disguises. I feel in my body today, as I write, the yearning and puzzling of the three-year-old son, and the two-year-old daughter.

I know as well that whiskey, work, consuming, being "entertained," indeed all passive stimulants, distance me from the child. Whiskey might be my devil, consuming as a leisure activity might be yours. We both have devils and the children are sorrowful.

The sorrow of the unfathered children can end with me.

A DAY OF MINDFULNESS

This is a day of retreat and renewal. Please see Appendix A.

There's no taking trout with dry breeches.
—MIGUEL DE CERVANTES

Comfort is pushed at us from every corner. We need to look critically at this comfortable society. We need to see what this comfort is taking from us. We need to consider the cost of this comfort. Perhaps we need to find another name for this comfort. Sloth? Indifference? Flight? Ignorance?

I was there when Willie was born. He was a large and robust baby. The birth was messy and hard. Pauline and I were face-to-face, inches apart as she pushed. We connected at a level of effort and trust that has marked our connectedness since. This was no time to be comfortable for either of us. It was not a time to pull out a camera to hide behind. It was not a time for me to be anywhere else. The sounds of that time, the great splash as Willie came to the world, his cries, and the doctor's sweet stern voice were not comfortable. Holding Willie to my chest, minutes later, was a time for awe, beyond celebration, and comfort won, not seized or bought.

Being a father is a messy business. A father's worries are like no other. Some of us have avoided these worries in disreputable ways. Our need for comfort, as we saw it, had heavy costs.

Today I will wade into the children's lives, unprotected.

A FATHER'S PRAYER

I know the children suffer in ways that I cannot always see. Today I pray that my eyes will be open and my heart strong. I pray that I will see what I have been afraid to see and that I will move to relieve the suffering.

Every aspect of our lives is connected to every other aspect of our lives. This truth is the basis for an awakened life.

—SHARON SALZBURG

When I am in my office writing, I am a father. When I am making breakfast for my children, I am a writer. When I am climbing in the Adirondacks, I am a cook. When I am working in my garden, I am a mountaineer. In every activity of my life, all other activities are present. The full awareness of this reality can bring a deep morality of each activity. When I am a father, I do not want to bring thief, liar, braggart, along. But if thief, liar, and braggart are present in my office, they are present in my fathering and they are easily seen.

The work of the spirited father is to see the connections fully and to be willing to lovingly disrupt and discard those aspects that taint the fathering.

I see that the father who yells at a careless driver brings the yelling home.

Real generosity towards the future lies in giving all to the present.

—ALBERT CAMUS

A perennial rock-and-roll star once said he wanted to be "used up" at the end . . . nothing left. The idea of being depleted, empty, every scintilla of good and of heart gone, is a foreign one. This is a "conserve-ative" era. Hold on. Look out. Be careful. Surf the net and avoid the eyes of the folks next door. In desperate efforts to conserve the heart, fathering is surrendered to the authority of strangers; the schoolmaster and the advertisers become the ethicists and the storytellers. The child and the father are lost, with dad holding on tight to everything but the child.

The spirited father is an openhearted creature: truthful, feeling, and captive of the muse. His open heart spends itsef outward to the entire universe and is faithfully replenished without a moment lost. He dances with the trees and laughs with the wind. He is the farmer, the wizard, and the charioteer. The child sees wild places in his eyes and feels surrounded by his strength. He wastes nothing and saves nothing.

Today I will use myself completely.

If we're not foolish young, we're foolish old.
—GEOFFREY CHAUCER

We are producing the most overorganized, time-sensitive, and fully occupied generation in recent history. We have Little Leagues, movie parties, theme parks, Boy Scouts, school teams, Girl Scouts, dance class, Sunday school, DARE, and therapists for every little asocial glitch. We make sure they are protected from mistakes or reproval.

If possible, we schedule our children right up to the moment of the rigid hug and obligatory kiss and a prayer to live through the night.

Perhaps we need to pray that our children dream the night through, in fields of purple marigolds under skies with a dozen suns and pastel rainbows. We'd better hope they get the kinks of our schedules out of their bones and muscles and run, free of our needs, in harlequin garb. Let's wish for them all the foolishness, mistakes, and hopeless giggles we deny them during the day.

Or let's make a bonfire of our schedules and brochures and dance, with the kids, on the ashes. Let's encourage chicanery, risk, and whispers behind our backs. Let's sit on the floor and make riddles and terrible jokes. Let's have take-out food fights and crush the fortune cookies with forceful slaps.

Let's have a parade to celebrate Today.

Be not hasty in thy spirit to be angry: for anger resteth in the bosom of fools.

—ECCLESIASTES 7:9

We think our anger is a thing. We believe it lives in us, with size, shape, and intent. We say, "I have a lot of anger" or "My anger is going to get me in trouble" or "My anger is justified." When this thing called anger presents itself, we identify with it. "I am angry."

Anger is not a thing. Anger is a habit.

One important thing to know about anger is that expressing it now enables us to express it more easily and more often in the future. Expressing anger creates only further expression of anger. It creates expressions of anger in ourselves and others. No one has ever said, "Thank you, I'll do as you suggest" in response to an angry demand.

Anger is a habit that breeds the habit of anger. It is not a thing.

Today when I am angry, I vow to stop and breathe deeply, returning to the present moment to heal the habit of anger.

Evil is unspectacular and always human,
And shares our bed and eats at our own table.
                                    —W. H. AUDEN

To do Evil is *merely* to cause pain or suffering. Evil is a powerful and jarring word and one we should not overuse. But we need to use it. It is a word that implies morality and ethics or, more properly, their lack. Evil is a theological word; it crackles with judgment and demands deep looking and change. To say, accurately, that this or that is an Evil thing or that Evil has been done in this place brings blazing light to the dark places, around us and in our souls.

In caring for the children, the father's job is to protect them from evil. Where is that evil? Where do we begin to look: down the block or across the planet? Where do we root out the evil? There must be a starting place.

If I wish to look to history to find evil, I need only to enter the stream of my own life. I don't need to turn on the TV and watch the so-called news, of parents who kill or madmen who bomb. I can simply look at my fear and weakness in dealing with my daughter, whom I didn't see for sixteen years. It has taken a lot of healing to eradicate that evil and the suffering it caused.

I am willing to see some of my past actions as evil, a new word for me. I can lovingly heal the hurt that evil has caused.

A DAY OF MINDFULNESS

This is a day of retreat and renewal. Please see Appendix A.

*. . . drinking steadily by the flames in the blackness,
that young man my father.*

—SHARON OLDS

My father drank when I was a boy. My greatest empathy is with the children of alcoholic fathers. It is a horror, mysterious and isolating. The sorrow these children feel is all the more horrible in their aloneness and massive ignorance. This is lion country. It's night with no moon.

But today I try to see that drinking is no better or worse than any of a myriad of death dances. Consuming is the problem. Thirst is the problem. "Fill 'er up," the father hollers. Alcoholism is the number one killer of middle-aged men in the United States. What if, just what if, we kept statistics on deaths of middle-aged men in the United States due to *consuming?* Look in the malls and restaurants and bars and the other temples. All the daddies dancing with Thanatos in conditioned air. Drunk. Oblivious. Cruel.

The dance is ending. Fathers are turning toward home. To "Heart, Hearth, Earth," in the words of trapeze artist Sam Keen. Surrounded by merchants of oblivion, we are seeking responsibility for the lives of children. Sober, engaged, and kind.

*Today I vow to turn my back to oblivion and dance the
dance the children teach.*

A FATHER'S PRAYER

*The children I know are surrounded by a world of exploitation.
The children I don't know live in the world of exploitation. In my
heart there is a profound ability to nurture and to move the children from a world of exploitation to a world of nurturance. Today
I pray that I will nurture and, by that simple act, create a world
of nurturance.*

Early this morning I walked out to the little pond in back of my house. The air was warm, the dew cool on my bare feet. I had just meditated for a while, in my office, with my dogs lying close to my black mat and cushion. I felt content as I walked.

As I approached the edge of the pond, a frog jumped *kerplop!* and I was touched by the spirit of the great poet Bashō whose frog jumped centuries before.

I enjoyed the "Today" show. My soul was enriched and I missed the news.

Today I will be open to the unexpected.

The heart is an awfully big place. It can hold a lot of people.

—RALPH SEVERSON

My wife is the last of five children. When her mother told her father that she was pregnant, he said, "I don't know if my heart is big enough." It was.

My daughter is twenty-five years older than my son. When I knew he was coming, I felt the empty space in my heart for the first time and felt it tremble with longing. It was filled.

I never knew my father-in-law, but I know many stories about him and I know our heart-feelings were the same. "How can I feel even more than I do—now I know only desire and uncertainty." Such a wonder that the uncertainties and strength of our hearts beat on, in his daughter, my wife, and his unknown grandson, my son.

Our greatest bond is our fear and our courage.

Today I will live with a growing heart.

*To love another you have to undertake some frag-
ment of their destiny.*

—QUENTIN CRISP

When a father can pitch himself, wholeheartedly,
into the life of his child, surrendering control and
in full mindfulness of the workings of destiny and
great unknowable powers, then he and the child are
fully in the flow of life. The spirited father can remind himself, daily, through prayer or secular sacra-
ment, that he is part of his children's destiny, not
its administrator. This is not a simple chore. There
is a cartoon I remember from childhood of a young
man in cap and gown, clutching his diploma, with
great academic buildings in the background, saying
to his parents, "Now may I run away and join the
circus?"

In mindfulness, the spirited father can listen
deeply to what the children are saying and to what
they are not saying. This requires great effort at
first, particularly for those who were never listened
to. If we look at our children with eyes of compassion, and listen with open hearts, and see our deep
kinship with them all, we will always do the right
thing.

*Today I will look at the mingling of my destiny with the
children's.*

A FATHER'S PRAYER

The world in front of my eyes is a place of wonder, if I look with the eyes of wonder. The world in front of my eyes is a place of joy, if I look with the eyes of joy. Today I pray for joy and wonder.

The past is not past. It is not even over.
—WILLIAM FAULKNER

The movie *Field of Dreams* is a great favorite of many men—a tale of baseball, nostalgia, healing, and magic. Many sons see in it the potential of healing, through magical means, the relationship with their fathers. It seems such a nice idea, this healing, and so completely in the realm of wishing. It exists only to remind us of what we don't have, or of what we missed.

In the practice of mindful living, such magic is ordinary. Each of us can have a catch with our twenty-five-year-old fathers if that's what we need. This is the truth. Sitting attentively, we can see our fathers as young men or even as toddlers if we wish, and we can play ball with them or hug them and give them our blessings.

Some fathers who practice this mindful living tell of unexpected moments of healing with many ancestors and go on to tell of the healing and the growth in their own fathering. This takes time and patience and constancy. Time and patience and constancy are bedrocks for the spirited father.

What we need is what we have.

We seem to have one near-life experience after the other.

—MARTHA DYSON

A great gift to give our children is our own *aliveness*! Aliveness, according to Brother David Steindl-Rast, is measured by degrees of awareness. He says as well, "That you have not died is not sufficient proof that you are alive."

What smell is in the air today, what sound drifts closest to the heart, what small and ordinary thing falls upon the eye and awakens the imagination to deeper understanding?

Is that a flower pushing through the stones?

What did the cicada say?

Who is making cinnamon rolls? How sweet they must taste.

Wake up!

It isn't enough for your heart to break because every-body's heart is broken now.

—ALLEN GINSBERG

Where in the world can we go? Where can we turn that there is not great suffering and sorrow? The lice and the scavengers are at us at every turn. Living with broken hearts, where do we take refuge?

Look deeply. Listen deeply. Find a moment with the one who fathered you when you knew comfort and connection. Savor it as you abandon yourself to it. How did that moment look, sound, taste, smell? What were your thoughts—if you had any?

Smile to that father and offer your blessings.

In this place where everybody's heart is broken, the child takes refuge in the wholehearted father. It is not enough to be brokenhearted! The spirited father strives to make his heart whole. That is enough.

Bless your heart.

A FATHER'S PRAYER

When I look at my children deeply I can see the strengths of my father and of all the fathers before him. Today I pray that I will honor the good in my father by honoring it in my child.

*A morning glory at my window satisfies me more
than the metaphysics of books.*

—WALT WHITMAN

The morning glory at the window contains a rich
history. Consider it.

Not the morning glory on this page. The one at
the window!

If there is no morning glory at your window, what
is there? Consider it. What is the life story of what
you see there. Look closely. What other hands have
brought it there? What weather, what celestial bodies, what plants, animals, minerals, and thoughts
have brought it to your windowsill?

Take your time.

What history is written at my window?

If you knew, as I do, the power of giving, you would not let a single meal pass without sharing some of it.

—THE BUDDHA

"I can give you things, including money, and that's good. I have enough to spare. It is more difficult to give you energy. I want to hold on to that energy, 'conserve' it, and make sure I have enough. So I will do what I can, but don't expect all of it. It is more difficult still for me to give you wisdom. To give you wisdom, I must trust myself, and I find that hard to do. I can give you my opinions, my attitudes, and my advice, but I have to hold back on the wisdom. Sorry, but you'll have to find wisdom somewhere else most of the time. Heh, heh. I just don't have much."

Could you say that, out loud, face-to-face, to a child?

Giving, to a child, a spouse, a family member, a co-worker, a stranger, or even to one we dislike, is a self-perpetuating act. It rolls on, accruing strength and breadth. As we let go of attitude and selfishness, we gain in the focused power of service. As we open-heartedly look and listen to the real needs of others, that which we give—material, energy, and wisdom—grows as fresh flowers grow in the space of the flowers that grew before them.

Today I will give recklessly.

A FATHER'S PRAYER

The child speaks to me from her soul when I listen with a quiet mind. The world caresses my own soul when I feel with a quiet mind. The life I share with the child is a life of blessings when I seek a quiet mind. Today I pray for a quiet mind.

A DAY OF MINDFULNESS

This is a day of retreat and renewal. Please see Appendix A.

*Truly, I say to you, whosoever does not receive the
Kingdom of God like a child shall not enter it.*
—LUKE 18:17

I was once in a mountaineer shop up in the Adirondacks getting some stuff to take Willie on a hike up Hurricane Mountain. The owner was helping us find some gaiters, boy-sized. He said that he'd better get used to looking for smaller sizes for his shop. I asked why and he said his first child had been born just the night before. I said, without thought, "Hey, your teacher has just been born. Look out."

It is a dangerous idea to sentimentalize what we might call *childmind*, but with caution it's a real good idea to look closely at what this mind has to offer.

Look Out!

Today I begin to see the child as teacher.

> *Developing the muscles of the soul demands no competitive spirit, no killer instinct, although it may erect pain barriers that the spiritual athlete must crash through.*
>
> —GERMAINE GREER

There are barrier gates a father must pass through if his fathering is to grow. There are not many measures. To become a spirited father is not an achievement. Our peers recognize us and love us, but they don't offer trophies, gold watches, bonus checks, or Havana cigars. Our partners don't make sandwiches and serve beer to the guys when we father well. When the pain comes, floating above fear, there may be support to break through, but the breakthrough is ours. At the very moment the barriers appear we are alone. One of mine was "I failed my daughter." Another was "Can I bear to watch my stepson be picked on, without turning aside or trying to 'save' him?"

The children know if the barriers defeat us. They see us turn to comfort and denial. They learn to do the same. If we offer our backs to the world, they learn the art of turning away. If we offer our anger to the world, they learn aversion and isolation. It's hard to be an openhearted father, facing the pain and doubt. It's harder still not to be one. If you doubt this, take a moment to see your soul—that is, your connectedness, your courage, your softness, your warmth. Do you see a wraith or a lion?

Today I will cultivate my soul.

*How refreshing, the whinny of a packhorse unloaded
of everything.*

       —ZEN SAYING—SOURCE UNKNOWN

What are you carrying there? How much of it do you need? I said *need*! If someone said, "Hey, what happened to all your stuff?" what would you say to her?

Unpack. Move in.

Dostoyevsky said we're all guilty of everything. And while I never could bring myself to accept Christian notions of sin and atonement, there's definitely something to karma. The things we do pile up on us, weigh us down. Or hold us in place, at very least.
—JAMES SALLIS

I remember coming back from a business trip, years ago, to my home in San Francisco. I was carrying a suitcase, briefcase, garment bag, plus two six-packs of beer and a quart of brandy. I had had the cab take me to a liquor store instead of home. I was already drunk and shaky from the night before. As I struggled up the hill toward my apartment building, I thought, "I've got too much stuff. I'm weighted down."

It was a sunny cool afternoon. The fog lurked above the distant hills to the south, ready to begin the stunning spill onto the beautiful city, ushering dusk and succor.

I count that day as the beginning of a spiritual awakening. A moment of clarity in what seemed a blighted life. I carried the weight of my actions. Mine; no one else's. For a moment there was no one to blame and I realized that I was not exempt! The law of karma applies equally. One of my teachers says that all we own are our actions. I began to see, meagerly, walking up Laguna Street that fall afternoon without the ability to express it, that all my actions have results. I was weighted down with my results—karma.

How much extra weight am I carrying?

A FATHER'S PRAYER

I pray that the children of this great earth will learn, through my example, that the earth is their home and that through my example they will see how to nurture it.

> . . . I would sometimes feel that a human being's life is not shaped so much by what he is or what he pretends to be or even by the compulsions that he tries to root out and burn away; instead it can be just a matter of a wrong turn in an angry moment and a disregard for its consequences.
>
> —JAMES LEE BURKE

It is reasonable to think that if I demand quick relief, quick reaction, quick thinking, and quick satisfaction, I will naturally give in to making that wrong turn in that angry moment. If I live my life distracted and half-asleep, lacking the gift of insight, I will naturally have little regard, in a quick minute, for what waits downstream from the trash I dump right here, unaware of where right here is.

Take heed. The long-term result is nothing you'll want when the cause is a short-term act of blind violence. Meditate today on the teachers of angry moments. Who teaches them to you, right now, today? How do these teachers get into your home? How do they get into your head? Are they palpable? Can you touch them, that is? Meditate as well on the teachers of "disregard." Who are they, right now, today?

Can you recognize the teachers, who sit in the corner, who you invite in?

Today I can look closely at the teachers of Ignorance and Anger.

The whole of life lies in the verb seeing.
　　　　　　　　　—TEILHARD DE CHARDIN

When a father looks at a child, he will sometimes begin to feel great fear and doubt. The future is clouded and haunted by spectral "haints" of ill health, bad times, loss, and pain. Out there ahead, he also sees, more with his gut's eye than his mind's eye, new freedoms, new knowings, and new associations. Consider this closely! When the father is seeing these things, he has entered the life of the child.

These moments are gifts of seeing deeply, and they can be sought through meditation and mindfulness. When a father says that he cannot know what is in the mind of a child, he is not thinking clearly. With an open mind, free of deluded thoughts of separation and of opinions of the way things "should be," the child and the father are one.

The father sees the child with the eyes of the child—not the eyes of a child but the eyes of that very child, right there!

In this very breath that we take now lies the secret that all great teachers try to tell us.
—PETER MATTHIESSEN

The only way that a father can look at a child is right here in the present moment. He cannot look at the child while he is somewhere else. Many times his child looks directly at him and knows that Daddy is not there. Daddy can be reading to the child and still be at work. Daddy can be sitting with the child and not feel her soft hand in his. The child sees that Daddy has not come home.

For the father to be home takes practice. It takes the practice of knowing how to breathe. More specifically, it takes the practice of knowing that he is breathing. *Breathing in, I know I am breathing in. Breathing out, I know I am breathing out. Present Moment, Only Moment.* When Daddy learns how to breathe, he will learn how to see.

Breathing in, I know I am breathing in. Breathing out, I know I am breathing out.

Love abides where all else dies
From sheer revulsion and disgust.
—HOWARD THURMAN

What are the teachings of love your children see in you? When you are with them in a city, do you take them quickly to the high places, away from earth and others? Do they see the aversion in you when a man or woman who suffers approaches? Do you teach them to stay away and say that we can't help them, they might move into our neighborhood? Or do you walk the streets with them? Do the children see you among others, compassionate and caring? Do you teach them to help by helping?

You have the seeds of love in you. No matter how repulsed you may be by the suffering all around, the repulsion is diminished as you water the seeds of love. Your fear of the pain you see in others will crumble as you water the seeds of love and kindness. Isn't that a gift you can easily give your children? Can't you let them teach you to reach out rather than to run away? Look at the children. They may show fear, but it is not yet "revulsion and disgust." Their love is still close to the surface.

My children will teach me not to turn away.

A FATHER'S PRAYER

I turn aside from awe in my cynicism. I know that when I am in awe of the vastness of creation, I can see the children in their wholeness. Today I pray for the reawakening of awe.

I understand now my true nature and know how to progress with developing my God-given talents.
　　　　　—CONFUCIUS (ON TURNING FIFTY)

At this moment I am fifty-four years old. I do not know that I am wise, but I do know that I am wiser than I was when I was thirty-three. However, whatever wisdom I may have did not lurk, fully developed, somewhere in my store consciousness, only to burst, scantily clad, from a cake on June 16, 1992. It developed, over time, and it is the part of consciousness to notice the incremental changes. It is the part, as well, of humility to understand that these changes are merely incremental.

For many of us, and certainly me, it is the part of youth to be neither conscious nor humble. So for those under fifty, I say have faith in absence of wisdom. For those over fifty, who have attained some wisdom rather than, say, a collection of mere things, I say have patience and gratitude. Especially have gratitude that you were given wisdom instead of baubles, and patience with the soft men who have only "stuff."

Today I see my gratitude, my patience, and my growing wisdom.

God does not have grandchildren.
—ANONYMOUS

Rest easy today in the knowledge that you are not in charge.

I give up.

A FATHER'S PRAYER

*Today I pray that those who act from greed will learn compassion.
I pray that those who act from anger will learn wisdom, and those
who act from ignorance will be enlightened.*

*We are the pain and what cures pain, both. We
are the sweet cold water and the jar that pours.*
—RUMI

Not one of us is merely anything. Consider the
thoughts that might roam about, behind your skin,
as you hold your child. If you look deeply into the
face of your child, who do you see? Do you see the
face of generations to come? Do you see the face
of your great-grandfather? Do you see the soil of
ancient lands, rich with becoming? Do you see the
face of God, and smell the breath of Mohammed?
Is that the hand of Shakayamuni Buddha himself
that circles your thumb? Is this child separate from
you and from all the ancestors? Is any child separate
from you and this child and all the ancestors?

Consider who is hurt if you hurt this child.

A DAY OF MINDFULNESS

This is a day of retreat and renewal. Please see Appendix A.

Yet why not say what happened?
—ROBERT LOWELL

There is no way out of the truth of our own lives. Lying about them, covering them up, simply adds a dissonant warp to the fabric. What is so horrible that we must never tell the children? What are they being protected from? Sure, all of us have done things we don't need to take on "Oprah," and most of us have done a few things that are best shared only with our closest partners. But what is the message to the child if we lie about how we felt that time we fell from the low branches of the tree when we weren't supposed to be there in the first place? What possible value is there in covering up past missteps? I have been married three times. My stepchildren and my son know this. I was in the army during the Vietnam era. I volunteered for Vietnam and was not sent. I have always felt as if a piece is missing. My children know this. What if I lied about my past entanglements or my military service? What would the children learn?

Do I teach truth or attitude?

It is when we insist most firmly on everyone else being "reasonable" that we become, ourselves, unreasonable.

—THOMAS MERTON

There is a Taoist parable of the man who wished to feed his monkeys four chestnuts in the morning and three chestnuts in the afternoon. The monkeys wanted three in the morning and four in the afternoon. When they challenged his plan (how is never explained), he simply did as they wished without argument. It is in this context that Merton asserts the above.

We don't get very far with the insistence that others understand and comply with our way of doing things. We can go great distances when we allow them to find their own way.

To tell a child that she is being "unreasonable" is really to tell her that she is being a child.

It is the part of greater wisdom to see the reason in her position. And greater wisdom still to allow her to follow her unreasonable instincts even when we do not understand! Our own foibles might be exposed.

When I insist that a child be "reasonable," I will try to remember that the emperor really was naked.

A FATHER'S PRAYER

I know that the children were originally kind. I pray today that the kindness they were born with will manifest again.

> . . . the only people for me are the mad ones, the ones who are mad to live, mad to talk, mad to be saved, desirous of everything at the same time, the ones who never yawn or say a commonplace thing, but burn, burn, burn like fabulous yellow roman candles exploding like spiders across the stars and in the middle you see the blue centerlight pop and everybody goes "Awww!"
>
> —JACK KEROUAC

This page is for Will Adams, a good man and a good father, who died too soon. We all knew a Will somewhere along the way.

What can you do in that man's memory today?

Will, I'll let the children know that I love them today.

If, after obtaining Buddha-hood, anyone in my land can't get ride hitch-hiking all directions, may I not attain highest perfect enlightenment.
    —GARY SNYDER (PUTTING WORDS IN
                   AMITABHA'S MOUTH)

Gia, my dear stepdaughter, now living in Israel, pointed out to me the other day that no one can hitchhike anywhere anymore. Even earlier in her few years, she could bum around on her thumb around town, and I went coast to coast in America several times and up and down the upstart twists and turns of California/Oregon/Washington a lot and even across Mexico and Central America.

Now neither of us would dare to stick out a thumb. Some bastard just might lop it off.

It's a sad task to list the delights of being young and free that are gone. When we are looking at the extinction of beings, plants, and minerals, maybe we should add the simple joys we knew not so long ago. Maybe if we see what our children can't do that we could, we'll get sad enough to do something about it.

Sitting on my cushion, waiting for enlightenment, I miss seeing what the children are missing.

The wise and moral man
Shines like a fire on a hilltop
Making money like the bee,
Who does not hurt the flower.
—THE PALI CANON,
SINGALAVADA-SUTTA,
DIGHA-NIKAYA

The banks and brokerage houses have replaced the mosques and synagogues in the centers of our cities. The lawyers have replaced the priests, the spin masters have killed off the poets. An air of "practicality" pervades our homes and schools. We learn and we teach social responsibility and the value of being a contributing member of society while politicians whimper about family values when what we mean is "contribute responsibly to the money machine and keep your nose clean."

All the while the children continue to die standing up or tumbling over.

So long as the pragmatic buck leads us, flowers will die. When the bucks happen as we nurture the flowers, harmony prevails and the air is scented with penetrating incense.

Consider for today what you want the children to learn. Merely to make money? To make money like the bee?

What do I teach about earning?

A DAY OF MINDFULNESS

This is a day of retreat and renewal. Please see Appendix A.

They will get it straight one day at the Sorbonne.
                    —WALLACE STEVENS

You know a lot more than you think . . . you know?

Today I'll trust my intuition.

Happy Unbirthday to Willie Alexander

Your pulse drives my blood.
The birth in winter of spring
Awakens all life.

Today I am grateful for life everlasting.

It's possible that the United States has achieved the first consistent culture of denial in the modern world. Denial can be considered as an extension—into all levels of society—of the naive person's inability to face the harsh facts of life.

—ROBERT BLY

"Hey, life's a bitch." "I'm hanging in there." "Good, I'm good." "Can't complain, how about you." "No problem."

A president said the country is in a funk and there is outrage. Listen. The country is in a funk. Here is a thesaurus for *funk*:

> Insanity: neurosis (noun)
> neurosis, psychoneurosis, anxiety neurosis, nerves, nervous disorder, neurasthenia
> hysteria
> attack of nerves, shattered nerves, nervous breakdown, brainstorm
> shell shock, combat fatigue
> obsession, compulsion, phobia, claustrophobia, agorophobia, PHOBIA
> hypochondria
> depression, depressed state, funk, blue funk, blues

Questions?
Here is the thesaurus for *naive*:

> Credulity: credulous (adjective)
> credulous, believing, persuasible, persuadable, amenable
> easily taken in, easily deceived, easily duped, GULLIBLE
> uncynical, unworldly
> naive, simple, unsophisticated, green
> childish, silly, soft, stupid, FOOLISH

A FATHER'S PRAYER

———— ✠ ————

Today I pray with all my being simply to be kind.

Not to transmit an experience is to betray it.
                                        —ELIE WIESEL

I have seen and done some things that perhaps I could have better avoided. I didn't, and those sights and actions are part of who I am. I was once witness to a scene of awful personal carnage—noise, shock, scent and sight of rifle shot and blood. Sounds of sirens and tires squealing were followed by the unforgiving pulse of red and blue cop-car lights outside my window. That experience changed me. I am not telling the details here because I do not believe that the transmission of an experience includes the right to betray another. This experience of mine taught me gruesome lessons. When the time is right—and I will easily recognize that time—it is my moral obligation to tell Willie about what happened. Until that time, I can empathize with the suffering of others only, and can work to end the causes of that suffering.

The experience I had all those years ago, as this happened not long after a young president was slain, and well before the children dared to dance in the streets, lives on in the present moment, and although I do not believe I had it for some *reason* imposed by an unreasonable God, I do believe that I can assign reason and significance to it.

My experience is the substance of my story and my stories.

A FATHER'S PRAYER

I get lost sometimes. I often have no idea where I am going and I lose sight of my true purpose. I know that if I simply look beneath my feet, I will see again the path I was on. Today I pray to find my way.

When making your choice in life, do not neglect to live.

—Samuel Johnson

Today and for the next few days, let's consider what this means: to live. Probably no one among us will, as death approaches, wish we had gone to the mall a few more times, or bought a better car or "retired" earlier. We are unlikely to miss having been lazy or greedy, that is.

If death is coming this afternoon, what will you do this morning?

It is not the same to talk of bulls as to be in the bullring.

—SPANISH PROVERB

If we look closely enough at our time, our busy minds and our actions and how they work together, we are liable to find dissonance. Our opinions rarely take up the least amount of time, in the forming, the articulating, and the expostulating. Our actions, born of those opinions, probably take little time at all. "The damned school isn't teaching the kids how to use their imagination! I'm going to go to the next meeting of that committee, *if I have the time*, and *listen* to what they have to say about it." How often is there time? Go to the next meeting of that committee. Count the fathers there. See how many of them say anything.

Then stop counting, stop watching, and say something.

Where do I put my involvement? Am I Living or talking?

Look at the View
Right to horizon
Talk to the sky
Act like you talk.
　　　　　　—ALLEN GINSBERG

Humbled by big sky, we talk in quiet voices, reverent, awe-filled, and yearning. The horizon of busy office building and filled sports arena, how puny under the big sky. How fragile our little homes, how delicate our beating hearts, seen under the big sky.

What would we talk to our children about, if we kept the horizon in view? Perhaps we would listen instead, with the horizon in view.

How would we talk to the teachers at school, if we kept the horizon in view? Perhaps we would praise them and fight for their rights, with the horizon in view.

Living today, I will see myself surrounded by the big sky, in proportion, and strive to stay right-sized.

I vow to offer joy to one person in the morning and to help relieve the grief of one person in the afternoon.

—THICH NHAT HANH

This vow is so concrete that it challenges us at a level far deeper than, say, "Our father . . . thy kingdom come . . ." Consider the effort, the faith, and the courage it will take to fulfill it. One person to whom joy is offered! One person whose grief is lovingly addressed! I can hear my teacher, John Daido Loori, saying, "Do it with your WHOLE BODY AND MIND!"

We are not accustomed to offering joy and comfort consciously. It takes uncommon effort to do these simple things. Consider, only for a moment please, what it might mean to take this simple vow each day and to fulfill it.

Then, if you can, Live it!

A FATHER'S PRAYER

I pray that the children will be safe today. I pray that I will look at the children with that prayer in my mind today. I pray that the children will be safe today.

I vow to live simply and sanely,
content with just a few possessions . . .
—THICH NHAT HANH

 T his is another fragment of the Refuge Prayer,
which was quoted earlier.

If you gave away everything you didn't need,
what would you have left? Consider the level of
contentment you feel as you become lighter.

Take it easy on yourself. It took years to accumu-
late all that stuff. It probably makes you feel secure
or successful. Are you secure? Are you successful?

Ask the children. They know your strengths.

Now look more deeply at your possessions, the
children's wisdom in your heart.

Where did all that crap come from?

A FATHER'S PRAYER

I pray to see the beauty of the children and to reflect it back to them. I pray to see the kindness of the children and to reflect it back to them. I pray to see the promise of the children and to reflect it back to them.

To set up what you like against what you dislike,
this is the disease of the mind.

—SENG TS'AN

It's my ideas about how things should be that cause me the trouble. Once "monkey mind" starts chattering, I cannot find peace. The house is too small or too big; I have too little money, time, space, imagination; or I have too much.

I know this is illusion. Unfortunately, the illusion usually leads me around with a hook through my nose, and then I decide there's something wrong because I can't let go of this very concrete illusion.

Then I have two problems. I have made up my mind that there is some problem of too much, too little, too pressing, or too distant, and then I decide that it's a problem that I create these problems. Do you see how it can go on? Do you see, just ahead there, a third possibility? "I don't like this and I don't like that I don't like it and I'm pissed that I don't like that I don't . . ."

They only way out of this one is through it.

Who put the mind in charge, anyway? Chattering little bastard.

We are monumentally distracted by a pervasive technological culture that appears to have a life of its own, one that insists on our full attention, continually seducing us and pulling us away from the opportunity to experience directly the true meaning of our lives.

—AL GORE

Here are some actions to take to break the trance:

> Start a poetry-writing group.
> Lie in the grass and have a tantrum.
> Offer joy to one person every day.
> Turn off the electricity and tell stories by candlelight.
> Let the phone ring three times before you answer it.
> Don't answer it.
> Watch television with the sound off. Make up dialogue.
> Go for a walk. Not a run, a walk!
> Bake bread.
> Make love.
> Play with a child.

The world is too much with us; late and soon,
Getting and spending, we lay waste our powers:
Little we see in nature that is ours,
We have given our hearts away.
> —WILLIAM WORDSWORTH

This is not a culture that rewards the contemplative and simple life. Not in this bloodied "first world," with its advertising industry and its manufactured spontaneity.

Can you stop and take a look at what the children are given, the stories they are told, the "products" they "consume," without sobbing?

Irony, the prevalent attitude of our day, is a pitiful response to the world we have made.

Sobbing and then striking the set should do very nicely.

Can you live in such a way as to recapture your heart and offer it to your children?

Today I can reclaim my heart.

There's a bird feeder just outside my office window—about six feet away from my busy hands. This morning there are chickadees and finches.

It snowed last night. The field beyond my porch is trackless, the snow is deep. At first light, the birds arrived. I had already been working for an hour.

The trees are still. No wind.

Present moment, wonderful moment.

The teenagers ain't all bad. I love 'em if nobody else does. There ain't nothing wrong with young people. Just quit lying to 'em.

— MOMS MABLEY

I have a bumper sticker on the bulletin board in my office. In familiar red script on a familiar black background it says "DARE—to think for yourself." This in a state that has bought the idea of drug education for its children with everyone but the children in mind. We're lying to 'em by telling them we're concerned. We're not concerned; we're scared silly!

We have built whole curriculums based not on the desire for our children to be kind and wise and clearheaded, but merely on the impoverished wish that they be functional, that they "contribute," i.e., that they produce and consume.

Can you sit down on the floor with your child, at her level, and tell her about a time you were scared and didn't get over it? Can you tell her you lied to her about something? Can you tell her you trust her to make the right decisions? Can you tell her that running away to join the circus sounds like a pretty good idea?

Can you tell your child you love her, without saying another word? Not one?

Our children are growing up now in an ethically polluted nation where substance is being sacrificed daily for shadow.
                              —MARIAN WRIGHT EDELMAN

Our children know what our ethics are no matter what we tell them. They understand full well what the ethics of our culture are without having to take a course. They know where the churches, temples, and mosques are simply by seeing where we spend our time. They know that shoes, haircuts, clothes, cars, and wristwatches make the man. They understand the virtues of indifference, impatience, and anger. They easily see that there is an *other* that is different and suspect.

Our children know what our ethics are no matter what we tell them. They understand full well what the ethics of our culture are without having to take a course. They understand that awe and wonder in the presence of power and beauty are good for the soul. They see deeply into the stories they are told, and feel, far better than we, the flow of story from future to present. They experience the virtues of humility, listening, and simplicity. They learn to build the circles that include.

Both of these statements are true.

What do I teach the children?

A FATHER'S GRATITUDE

In the presence of my child I am grateful for the gifts she brings to me.

———————

Aware of the pain caused by harshness
Today I vow with every living thing
to speak gently and softly
and to listen deeply and kindly

———————

A DAY OF MINDFULNESS

This is a day of retreat and renewal. Please see Appendix A.

Aware of the joy caused by gentleness
Today I vow with every living thing
to touch the peace within myself
and within all about me

Aware of the suffering caused by greed
Today I vow with every living thing
to live simply
and consume mindfully

Aware of the joy caused by simplicity
Today I vow with every living thing
to consume less
and give more

_____

Aware of the suffering caused by noise
Today I vow with every living thing
to cease from loud speech
and create silence as I go about my living

_____

Everything in nature invites us constantly to be what we are.

—GRETEL EHRLICH

I was mighty uncomfortable with the idea of a Sky God from the time that I was president of a youth fellowship at a Presbyterian church in Nashville until many years later when I was confronted, at soul level, with the unmistakable evidence that I was not in charge here. There was clearly some power, greater than myself, that moved in time, space, and being. I was certain, at least, that this power was not male, not someplace, not opinionated, and not a fantasy. I was equally certain that it did not, not have the qualities of maleness, location, inquiry, and imagination.

Then I read the story of the Zen master who, when a student asked about this power, pointed out the window at a great volcano in the distance and told him that if he needed to see a power greater than himself, he had only to look at that volcano and know "the power of things as they are."

Now when I am surfing or mountain-climbing, or simply looking out my window at the fields of snow in deep winter, I am reminded of a power greater than myself. I also know this power when Willie says, "Dad, I need a Plum Village Hug," and I know it when I read of the horrors of the world.

*The power of things **as they are** is a power greater than myself.*

A DAY OF PRACTICE:
Plum Village Hugs

I have spent time at Plum Village, a meditation center in southwest France, founded by Vietnamese Zen master, poet, and peace worker Thich Nhat Hanh. I learned many things there, about myself, about Zen practice, about "the power of things as they are."

One practice I brought into my life is the practice of Hugging Meditation or, as we know it in my family, Plum Village Hugs. This is a very healing practice and I want to share it with you.

You may request a Plum Village Hug from your friend by means of a simple bow or by saying, "I need a Plum Village Hug." When he agrees, with a bow or a smile, you embrace each other, gently and fully. You stand, close together, without moving, without slapping each other on the back, without little extra squeezes. You just stand there and breathe together (CON-SPIRE) for three deep breaths. No more, no less. Then you step apart, bow, and smile.

This is a very challenging and healing practice.

Today is a day to practice Plum Village Hugs.

Great men are they who see that spiritual is stronger than any material force, that thoughts rule the world.

—RALPH WALDO EMERSON

What will you teach your children about the way they work? In a psychologized, fundamentalist, materialist age, will you prescribe therapy, prayer, or pills for what bothers them?

Or will you look more deeply, not at the cure but at what bothers them? If they are not fitting in or are marching to a very different drummer, could you see that as spirit? Can you let go of the idea of "dysfunctional," which is machinelike, and embrace the reality of spirit?

If they are seeking understanding of their roots, will you tell them about family and genetics? Or can you include myth and story?

Do you confuse them by equivocating about God or gods? What do you tell them about the world of spirit?

I can teach the eternal.

A FATHER'S GRATITUDE

When I consider deeply what it means to be a father—caring, kind, nurturing—I offer my gratitude for this destiny.

There was a child went forth every day,
And the first object he look'd upon, that object he
became.

—WALT WHITMAN

Can you walk into the world today with your child, and make the effort to see what she sees? That is, when she is on the tire swing, can you enter into the awe and wonder of swinging high above the brilliant green grass, with its valleys and hidden places, and, upward to the great sky, golden and full of life?

Can you walk slowly, alone on the sidewalk, and see the earth falling away on either side? Can you see the flowers and not know the names of the colors?

Can you wonder at the swirls and various colors in the skin at the end of your finger? Can you fall into it, body and mind forgotten?

CHILDMIND!

Art washes away from the soul the dust of every-day life.

—PABLO PICASSO

What is your art? Do you write little poems, draw caricatures, bake croissants on Sunday?

We are going to spend a few days looking at arts—no quibbling here; the art of business or the art of child rearing doesn't count for these little discussions. No easy outs, that is to say.

What is the art you are going to practice. Drawing? Writing poems? Building birdhouses? Doing calligraphy? Playing a flute or whatever instrument you played all those years ago? Playing a harmonica or whatever instrument you wanted to play all those years ago?

Today I will concentrate on choosing an art. Making that choice will consume and distract me all day.

A DAY OF MINDFULNESS

This is a day of retreat and renewal. Please see Appendix A.

Art is I, science is we.
—CLAUDE BERNARD

Doing your art can be a daily endeavor, perhaps during your quiet time in the morning, before the rest of your world comes to call. You can do your art as you are walking to work, the way a great American poet did, concerning yourself with imagination, just as he did. You can do your art in the kitchen while everyone else is being entertained in some other room. What is most important is to know that you are doing it alone.

Savor this time with your pen, your brush, or your instrument.

No one is watching.

I'm the only one here.

Everyone is as God made him, and often a good deal worse.

— MIGUEL DE CERVANTES

If you are trying to do your art perfectly, you are already failing.

What is the aim you have in mind?

Abandon it!

The time for doing your art is the time for doing your soul. This is loving, easy work, born out of a simple desire to fill some God-shaped holes here and there.

Please, don't bring your fear in here. Bring only your caring.

If I don't do my art perfectly today, I'm doing it perfectly.

Without this playing with fantasy, no creative work has ever yet come to birth. The debt we owe to the play of imagination is incalculable.

— CARL GUSTAV JUNG

What can you imagine? Can you build a home for your six-legged fish? Can you be sure that the puppies turn the light out before they clean the corral? Is your poem still in the garage?

Our demands to be entertained are leaking the life out of our imaginations. We sit passively at the TV altar and squander the riches of fantasy, visualization, metaphor, and dream weaving.

We have "lifestyles" rather than lives. Our clothes are costumes and our homes are stage sets. Figuring out a new way to spend money is not imagination—it is fear of dying. In our depression we are left with a world imagined by marketers and cynics. There is not much imagination there.

Imagine that . . .

A FATHER'S GRATITUDE

The sky boils about me and the earth is firm beneath my feet. In moments of uncertainty, I am fed and supported by a power greater than myself. It is always there, and for that I am grateful.

Ink runs from the corners of my mouth.
There is no happiness like mine.
I have been eating poetry.
　　　　　　　　—MARK STRAND

On New Year's Eve, maybe it was 1971 or maybe 1972, I went to a party with Mark Strand. I was wearing a leather jacket with bone buttons; he was wearing a very tweed jacket. The party was on the Upper East Side of Manhattan. We stood off to the side, mostly, and gabbed.

There was a roast beef and there were cherry tomatoes and dip with chives and sour cream. There was no music playing, but the voices hummed and sang. We talked about translations and blood.

I soon moved to California. Mark, I hear, moved to Utah.

The taste of that New Year's Eve is still sweet.

Taste a day, from years ago.

If a nation loses its storytellers, it loses its childhood.
                                        —PETER HANDKE

Consider who the storytellers are. Is it possible that we have lost our storytellers while we pretend that we have many? Think of the "stories" you remember from your childhood. Who told them? I only remember the story of one movie, and that was *Bambi*!

I well remember the stories my mother and father told of their lives and their families' lives in Mississippi and Tennessee. I remember my uncle's stories of being in war and I remember the story of a great-great-uncle I never knew whose notched-barrel rifle from the Civil War hung above the bed where I slept, in summer, on the porch off the dining room in small-town West Tennessee.

What stories do your children know? Do they have their blood running in them?

I am my children's best storyteller. Without me, their childhood is barren.

We have kept our children so busy with "useful" and "improving" activities that we are in danger of raising a generation of young people who are terrified of silence, of being alone with their own thoughts.
—EDA J. LESHAN

In my home we have an hour of silence in the late afternoon, before dinner. This is a time only to be quiet. It is not naptime, homework time, or quiet playtime. Sometimes the children—there are four of them—sit in meditation for a few minutes. Sometimes they read. Sometimes, it seems, they just "simmer," that is, they process the day, letting go or filing their experience of the previous few hours. They are learning the art of Doing Nothing. (Dinner is such a peaceful affair.)

The children, and I, can learn to Do Nothing every day.

A DAY OF MINDFULNESS

This is a day of retreat and renewal. Please see Appendix A.

Real education should educate us out of self into something far finer—into selflessness which links us with all humanity.

—NANCY ASTOR

As fathers we need to remember that our children need more than mere proficiency and a dulling knowledge of how to do some one thing. As we participate in their education, we need to encourage and support the wildness and heedless inquiry they are so abundantly capable of acting on. We must be careful not to let the educators suffer from the illness of narrow ends and narrow means.

From the beginning, childmind, wild mind, is connected. It is a dangerous error to think that disconnecting is useful. It is not. Only the journey into self-awareness as a way out of self is useful. Wild mind pervades the whole universe. Tamed mine goes meekly to the water cooler.

These are wild minds we are dealing with here. It is not the purpose of education to tame them but to let them run. When our schools are doing otherwise, we must go wild ourselves. We must see that the connection the children learn is to all of humanity, in its chaos and joy, rather than to limited self-interest.

Today I can consider what is being taught to the children I love.

It is the privilege of adults to give advice. It is the privilege of youth not to listen. Both avail themselves of their privileges, and the world rocks along.

—D. SUTTEN

The children certainly don't hear what we say they should do very often. That's their job. However, they do see what we do and they are deeply aware of the difference between what we say they should do and what we do ourselves.

"Money is not the most important thing. Learn to enjoy the world around you," we say on Thursday.

"There's nothing to do. Let's go shopping. Maybe we'll find something we need," we say on Saturday, with the first birds of spring pecking at the hard ground just outside the kitchen window.

It is a little arrogant to assume the children won't listen at all. I think the reality is that they won't listen for long to hypocrites.

Saying, "Drink tea" while I'm swilling gin just won't play.

A DAY OF MINDFULNESS

This is a day of retreat and renewal. Please see Appendix A.

A FATHER'S GRATITUDE

Those I love are safe when I see that their safety does not rest only with me. I am humbly grateful for the safety of those I love.

Start Where You Are.
　　　　　　　　—PEMA CHODRON

Start at home. Whatever it is you want to be sure the world does, start it at home. Nowhere else.

Where else is there? Point to someplace other than where you are and where you can start something. Now start it there. Consider this carefully.

I simply cannot put an end to war anyplace other than right where I am. That place is the source of war, anger, fear, exploitation, and isolation. That place is where it all begins.

Where does it end?

You can't think and hit at the same time.
—YOGI BERRA

When we are caring for our children, we need to put down the book and pick up the child. I am sure that many fathers, like me, have had the experience of thinking they don't know how to do any number of things and then discovering that they are hard-wired for the task when they give up fretting and simply follow their instincts. I broke that barrier the night Willie was born. Minutes after his birth, the doctor told me to pick him up and bring him to Pauline. She didn't ask me if I wanted to, she told me to do it. I did. I knew exactly how to hold him and I crooned comfort to his ear from a very deep part of me. That was the end of not "knowing" and the beginning of simply acting, in response to centuries of learning.

I can surrender to the nurturing instinct, no matter the age or needs of the children.

One must think like a hero to behave as a merely decent human being.

—MAY SARTON

Men are trying to be good parents at a time when the larger culture does not understand good parenting. There is a great deal of talk, from politicians and corporations, about support for parents, but we shouldn't be so willing to accept a dollar from a man who wants $1.25 back. I want to do the best for my children; to love, support, encourage, and nurture them. They are surrounded by forces that wish to exploit them. Betty Friedan said that the problem that men have today is that there are no more bears to be killed. I don't believe this. The bears are harder to see, but there is plenty of killing to be done.

Consider the health of the planet. Consider the wars and violence. Consider whether you know your neighbors. Consider where your water comes from. Consider where your money comes from.

It is not so easy to be a decent parent without being a hero after all. And there are bears everywhere, even in the family room.

Today I can practice the heroism of the decent human being.

The more we understand individual things, the more we understand God.
            —BENEDICT DE SPINOZA

It is so difficult, immersed as we are in a speed-obsessed technological culture, to understand even the smallest things. We discover, however, that as we begin to look closely at the most mundane and ordinary things, we begin to see a greater wonder. The problem, for one example, is not just that many of us avoid the natural world, but that even when we are in it, we don't see it. When we miss the wonder of discrete units of a larger beauty, we miss the larger beauty. Willie and I sat by a brook in the Adirondacks one summer afternoon, eating chocolate and raisins and drinking cool water. Insects danced in the sunlit dust motes. Birds sang and water rustled. Willie and I moved, for a while, in the greater dance. I came away with a deeper understanding of our simple connection. That is all that I can relate here, but I know that there is more, unremembered and unforgotten, that Willie and I carry.

Look! There's God, right there. Pay attention.

When you are dealing with a child, keep all your wits about you, and sit on the floor.
—AUSTIN O'MALLEY

My father towered over me when I was a boy. Even as I became older and passed him in size, when he sat in his chair at his desk, he was so big, so far away, so hard to look in the eye. I miss having had with him what we have with our kids: the illusion, at least, of being of equal size. Whenever it's time to talk about the important stuff in this family, we "go to the floor." Lizzie was the first to put it that way, and that's the way it still is. Sitting on the floor with the children, in emotional fair or foul weather, levels us out. I don't know how they feel about it, really, but I know that I feel softer and kinder.

My generation asked, "Where are you coming from?." "The floor" is the best answer I've known.

I'll be child-sized today.

Providing for one's family as a good husband and father is a water-tight excuse for making money hand over fist.

—EVA FIGES

We lived in Manhattan for quite a few years. In our neighborhood, wealth and disease walked together. Here is something I saw there. A limousine, black and gleaming, pulled up in front of our children's school, not parking, but stopping in the street, blocking crosstown traffic, while the driver got out and walked back to the rear to open the door for the passenger. The passenger was a five-year-old girl. She hopped out and ran into the school, the driver returned to his station, the limo pulled away, traffic resumed.

Someone had taught that poor child to wait until the door was opened. And don't blame it on traffic. There wasn't any!

Exploitation of anyone to support our children is an unfathomable sin. They are marked by it and they will hate us for it.

What do I provide?

> *I say me, all the while knowing it's not me.*
> —SAMUEL BECKETT

I used to live in the East Village in New York City, back in the late sixties. I had two friends who scavenged the uptown neighborhoods for furniture, tossed on the sidewalk once a week for pickup. One Thursday night I ran into them on St. Marks Place just as they were getting in their van to go on their rounds. I had a new apartment on Avenue A and needed furniture. I asked if they would hold some good pieces back for me, you know, check with me before their regular "customers." They said OK, reluctantly, and as I headed on east I heard one of them say, "Me, me, me, me, me."

That was a lesson that has continued to sink in for nearly thirty years. At first it was about selfishness only, but now I see it differently. Me, me, me is about illusion; an illusion that I can't live without but that must always be kept conscious.

I ain't me, babe.

> *[The other is]* the one you can't recognize as being like you.
>
> — JEAN-CLAUDE CARRIÈRE

I am made up entirely of non-me elements. As Whitman said, "I contain multitudes." There is no one outside of me. I understand, in an intimate way, the infinite interplay of all of us, the great web of sentient beings who touch each other at every moment. When I look at you, I can see myself and all of our ancestors.

If I turn away from you, because you don't meet my ego-driven requirements for inclusion, I am dismembering myself. I have learned this by doing it, and it has been my children who have pointed out my smugness and egocentricity. Between my father's lingering illness and my children's point-blank honesty, I have been forced to a position of heartfelt connection with Other. Other disappears.

Who is this Other?

[Compassion is] first of all, a fact.
                                        —THE DALAI LAMA

Then compassion is not a feeling. Compassion is not isolated from or directed toward anything. We do not develop compassion. We "realize" it. It is always there. We are a part of this earth and related to everything on it, intimately. Compassion then describes the great reality of interconnectedness.

I choose to believe this. It makes sense out of my occasional sorrow at the state of things, it puts a finer edge of my joy, and it makes charity inevitable.

I can see the fact of my life as compassion.

A FATHER'S GRATITUDE

Today I offer my gratitude for the village that supports me in raising the children. This gratitude will not go unexpressed.

Those who seek to satisfy the mind of man by hampering it with ceremonies and music and affecting charity and devotion have lost their original nature.
—CHUANG-TZU

W hat might this mean today? Old Chuang-tzu might have been talking about the Confucians of his day, but we can look at more than the churches, temples, and synagogues. We are surrounded by ceremony, music, affectations of charity and devotion to *satisfy* our minds, which finally only fog and destroy them. "Those who seek . . ." today are not only churchmen and teachers, they are the politicians, dilletantes, and popinjays of marketing and Instant Relief. Chuang-tzu says they have lost their original nature. What is that nature? I suggest that it is the realization of compassion. Then satisfaction is an inside job.

Today is a day of inner satisfaction.

Our limitations serve, our wounds serve, even our darkness can serve.

—RACHEL NAOMI REMEN

It is crucial that we offer our wholeness to the children. My father could not swim. He was in the navy during WWII, on board ship for part of the time, and was once swept overboard on a training maneuver off Key West. He was dragged from the ocean, intact. He loved to tell that story and did so without shame or embarrassment. He also never failed to go into the water when we took family vacations, in the fifties, at Daytona Beach. Once, when I was about age nine, he and I were on the sandbar offshore when an unexpected wave hit, dumping Dad on the deep side of the bar. I grabbed his hand and held on while he struggled back to the ankle-deep water and firm sand. He was frightened, but after wiping his face, combing his fingers through his hair to straighten it, and taking several deep breaths, he shook his head ruefully and thanked me.

The important thing to me about that story is that Dad was always willing to go into the water, admitting that he couldn't swim. He didn't lie about that, just like many years later, when he told me of other, deeper problems that he saw we both shared. Because of his openness in the past, I was willing to listen in those moments of my own drowning.

I can share my wholeness with the children.

It's a lot worse to be soul-hungry than to be body-hungry.

—ANONYMOUS—ATTRIBUTED TO A KENTUCKY WOMAN TRYING TO GET HER GRANDDAUGHTER INTO SCHOOL CA. 1900

Our task as dads is often to put something on the table that is inedible. We need to serve up platters of ideas, questions, riddles, and challenges. I have had children say to me that their parents *only* buy them stuff, when what they really want is just to be with them, hanging out, talking and getting to know them. I am sad when I see the dads who are so frightened that all they can do is grill the steak on Saturday afternoon, when they could be hunkered down in the dirt, side by side with the child watching an ant carry a crumb over wisps of straw and clumps of mud.

How do I feed the soul?

> It's not the frivolity of women that makes them so
> intolerable, it's their ghastly enthusiasm.
> —HORACE RUMPOLE (VIA JOHN MORTIMER)

Take a look at your reaction to this one.

I think it is wickedly funny; deflating, asynchronous, and delicious.

I see that it is sexist, irreverent, and demeaning.

I hope I will never stop laughing at such winsome thoughts and I hope that I will never take them, or myself, too seriously.

Lighten up.

Do not mistake a child for his symptom.
                              —ERIK ERIKSON

I'm an alcoholic. That is not who I am or even all of what I am. It is not my identity and I will become extremely difficult with anyone who chooses to see all of me filtered through a small glass. To the same degree, I need to be particularly careful not to see any of my children, or any children, as their symptom. One child close to me is troubling, and I must struggle to see him in his wholeness. I live in the country; ghetto kids are foreign to me, but I must never see them as their symptoms as presented in the popular culture. I am Caucasian, and although I also have a Vietnamese name, given me by a Buddhist teacher, I must be careful not to see the children of Asia as their symptoms, as presented by either a maudlin or jingoistic culture. My job is to see the child in her wholeness and to serve, with awe and wonder.

Today I will look through the symptoms to the child.

> *If a child is to keep alive his inborn sense of wonder . . . he needs the companionship of at least one adult who can share it, rediscovering with him the joy, excitement and mystery of the world we live in.*
>
> —RACHEL CARSON

Is it possible for you to go into the world with a child today, or with, at the least, a child's mind, in preparation for the joy of taking the trip with the delight of a child by your side? What does it take to "rediscover" the "joy, excitement and mystery of the world we live in"?

Go slowly. Look down, up, and to the sides. Use your nose for seeing, your eyes for hearing. Enter with the child the awe of the not knowing what you are seeing. Become lost in the wonder of it. Shimmer in the wind with the green and silver leaves. Listen. The frogs are beginning to talk.

Soon, the crickets.

Wonder.

A FATHER'S GRATITUDE

———— ✥ ————

Today I will consider my partner deeply and see all of the ways that this person and I work together. When I can truly understand all that is done by my partner, I am grateful.

Dictators ride to and fro upon a tiger from which they dare not dismount.

—HINDU PROVERB

The father who will not share the truth of his life, who says "because I said so" either in fact or in manner, and whose means of keeping order are through intimidation and punishment is in a narrow corridor, and the door at the end is locked from the other side. Most often their children know how to get their way, surreptitiously, and have no respect for the tyrant down the hall.

Saddest of all, this father is denying himself, through his autocratic and selfish style, the warmth of his children. He is too mean to be seen as tragic, too grand to appear the fool. He is simply isolated from the reality of his family and he serves them poorly or not at all.

My place is on the floor.

Fathers, do not provoke your children, lest they become discouraged.

—COLOSSIANS 3:21

One of fatherhood's tasks is to encourage the child. To give her courage to move through difficulties and uncertainty while allowing her to move awkwardly and with varied successes. It is too easy to discourage her by saying don't do that, that's stupid, that's too much for you. Another synonym for *provoke* is *vex*. When a child is told that she should not do or have done this or that, she is vexed: bewildered and thrown into self-doubt.

Most parents encourage a child to walk, and then fall into telling her not to go anywhere. She's going to trip again, time after time after time. If she is provoked when she tries, the only lesson, finally, will be not to try. The tightrope walker will never leave home.

I can encourage the child by letting her fail.

A competitive society is a society of envy.
—DOROTHEE SOLLEE

I have noticed, among some children, an understanding of connection to one another and to a larger world that I did not see when I was a child. The schools make, for the most part, an impoverished attempt to make sense of this connection, and few parents seem to understand it at all. But I am heartened when I see kids who are loyal, who put back in the earth that which came from it, who choose to practice charity through service rather than through mere fixing or helping.

How is it that these children, surrounded by exhortations to produce and consume, that is, to be just like their parents, somehow can put it aside and treasure the personal, the worn-out, and the intimate? Have we perhaps gotten to a point of envy overload? Has there finally been one too many mean-spirited politicians, or corrupt sports heroes, or greedy family members, and the mold just cracked from overuse? I don't know the answer to these questions for sure, but I do know that I will encourage cooperation and look away from competition at every turn.

I won't play the game. I'll join in the dance.

A DAY OF MINDFULNESS

———— ✦ ————

This is a day of retreat and renewal. Please see Appendix A.

If we could read the secret history of our enemies, we should find in each man's life sorrow and suffering enough to disarm all hostility.

—HENRY WADSWORTH LONGFELLOW

My foulest enemy is still more like me than he is different from me. When I demonize him, I am cutting off a part of myself and throwing it into the gutter. When I tell the children what I hate, they learn to hate that in themselves! Dad says it's hateful and it's in me, so there is part of me that is hateful and corrupt.

At every moment, when I begin to see the enemy, I need to look more deeply and find myself in him.

There is no enemy but in my mind.

No sooner are the lips still than the soul awakes, and sets forth on its labors.
— MAURICE MAETERLINCK

Incessant activity and a life lived in surround-sound, no matter now purposeful and virtuous, is in trouble without regular retreats to silence. This is the silence not necessarily of surroundings but of the dedication of the entire being to no-sound, within or without. It is possible, rather, necessary, to walk the city streets in silence and repose. Let the soul do its work in every circumstance. Meditation is not something that takes place only on a cushion or in a monastic environment. The power of meditation is available at every moment.

Today I'll walk silent streets, mouth and mind quiet, soul at work.

Is it progress if a cannibal uses a fork?
                    —STANISLAW J. LEC

The thoughtful father sees the lie of progress. Faster, newer, easier, bigger, and all those nuthouse words are about scale, efficiency, and duration. They are not about value, but are often mistakenly thought to be so. The world our children live in and are liable to inherit is not the place we saw, even ten years ago.

There is no going back. Few of us are going to move to remote homes and live off the grid. Indeed, that is often a spiritual conceit, another form of consumerism, another fork for another cannibal. We are on a path of no turning back, and *if we make it*, it will be because we have regained our spiritual imaginations and learned again to question, question, question, relentlessly, the value of the new, the fast, the easy, and the big.

Our children don't need those toys we buy for ourselves. They need a touch, a quiet word, and an introduction to the value of the spirit.

Today I can ask myself what is of value that I see.

A FATHER'S GRATITUDE

*I will visit the children as they sleep tonight and silently offer my
gratitude for their lives.*

*The truth is, it is not Jesus as historically known,
but Jesus as spiritually arisen within men, that is
significant for our time, and can help it.*
                                    —ALBERT SCHWEITZER

Willie, at age six, became concerned that Jesus
had had such a short life. He told me that it wasn't
fair that a man who "only taught love and peace"
should die so young. But then he thought some
more and said that he guessed that Jesus wasn't really dead because we still think about him. I agreed
with that and pointed out that the Buddha had lived
and died five hundred years before Jesus, and we
still remembered him and his teachings. Willie went
on, "So Jesus knew Buddha, didn't he?" I told him no,
that five hundred years passed between the Buddha's
death and the birth of Christ. "Dad," he said, in that
tone that every father knows, full of exasperation
and tenderness, "Jesus knew Buddha in his heart,
because they both taught the same things!" "Yep,"
I said.

I hugged him, and he gave his soccer ball a powerful kick and followed it, full tilt, out of the room.
Me and Jesus and the Buddha sat in awe for a while.

Where is Jesus today?

The young are looking for living models whom they can imitate and who are capable of rousing their enthusiasm and drawing them to a deeper kind of life.
—BAKOLE WAS ILUNGA

That children are looking for models is no mystery, and these days there is an endless line of eager marketers and hapless folks, caught momentarily in the spotlight, who will provide them. We need to be certain that we know what needs to be modeled. J. D. Salinger, Jack Kerouac, and John Lee Hooker did it for me. Bill Russell, too. These were mystics, in my mind, and I was not from a family that countenanced mysticism and did not grow up in a time when such pursuits had risen to the top of the brew. Nonetheless, they pointed me to a "deeper kind of life." With the exception of Kerouac, not one of those guys had any mystical pretenses, and yet they shined with it.

We need to consider the role models the young have today. Are they pointing at a deeper kind of life? Some are, I think. Some sports figures and some entertainers, the quiet ones who do not advertise their virtues, seem to have the shine. Others only have the glitter. Our job is to see the difference.

Where are the children being drawn?

Unformed people delight in the gaudy and in novelty. Cooked people delight in the ordinary.
—ZEN THOUGHT—ANONYMOUS

It is in the wonder of the present moment at the center of our lives that we are most free. Only in the midst of the ordinary do we live with fire and purpose.

The kids are unformed, forming.

The spirited father lives in the world of this and that, seeing the sacred in the ordinary.

Can we learn to leave the gaudy and the novel to the kids? We are enjoined to "put aside childish things," but many of us don't. The children suffer when the father must be amused and entertained by the gaudy and the new. It is not only his own children who suffer, but the children of all the world and the children of generations to come. The spirited father must consider the larger costs of his cars, his cigars, and his eighty-dollar shirts.

Who suffers from my childishness?

*You are part of the infinite. This is your nature.
Hence you are your brother's keeper.*
—SWAMI VIVEKANANDA

I was out for an early morning run in Central
Park. It was dark still, and the air held the cold of
late winter. I pounded on alone, aware of distant
city sounds, absorbed in my breath and my random
and fragmented thoughts. There were other runners,
but we didn't take much notice of each other.

As I approached a smear of light beneath a lam-
post, I saw a familiar face coming toward me. My
friend Richard, a marathoner, was out for his training run. As we came closer we locked eyes and
smiled, and just at the right moment, we threw up
our left arms and slapped a perfect high five, without
breaking stride or saying a word.

That was a breakthrough moment for me. For the
rest of my run I felt a tingle of connectedness that
had been foreign to me. I can summon it today,
when I try.

I think we must open ourselves to the *possibility*
of being connected, of being our brother's keeper,
in order to realize it. Locked in our greed, aversion,
and ignorance, we cannot feel this greater truth.

Am I my brother's keeper? How would I know?

And everything comes to one, as we dance on, dance on, dance on.

—THEODORE ROETHKE

Imagine this. You are walking a crowded city street. Everyone rushes, steam pours from the sidewalk, taxi horns blare, vendors push their wares. The more you walk, the more difficult walking becomes. Everyone is an adversary as openings appear and quickly close. You are increasingly frustrated; the man in front of you is so slow, the kid can't walk in a straight line, you'll never make the light, and the cabbies are morons.

Imagine that you grab someone in a tender stance and begin to waltz. Imagine that all stops for an instant and then that everyone begins the waltz, with partners or without.

The whole damned city dances. The cabs rear up on their back wheels and do a gavotte. The buildings ever so slowly sway in time and the air crackles in rhythm. You dance on to your destination, transformed by the dance.

This is what happens.

Woe to us human beings of the 20th Century, that we have seen innocent children pay for the mistakes of adults.

—ELIE WIESEL

What can you do, today, about all the children we have killed, and to protect the children still alive? There is a great deal to be done. Picket the manufacturers of land mines. Support legislation to outlaw guns. Volunteer at a shelter or clinic. Hold an AIDS baby. Stay home from work and play with your children. Quit your most destructive addiction.

Mourn and ask others to mourn with you. Be silent all day in memory of the children who have died just in the past twenty-four hours. Scream with rage. Pray formally, in a place of prayer.

Do in your home what you think should be done in the world to honor the dead and protect the living children.

What can you do today?

We have forgotten who we are.
We have sought only our own security
We have exploited simply for our own ends
We have distorted our knowledge
We have abused our power.
—UN Environmental Sabbath Program

There is the world of exploitation and there is the world of nurturance. Each of us, each day, at every moment, can make the choice to live in one or the other. A moment's reflection before action is often all that is necessary. Reflection is the antidote to exploitation and ignorance. As kids, we were taught to count to ten; now we can count to ten while reflecting on the nature of our actions.

Will what I want to do right now harm the children? Will what I want to do right now feed another or feed my ego? Will this action serve or exploit? There are so many reflective questions that will push aside ego-driven exploitation and draw us closer to nurturing and understanding.

What question can I ask, in reflection, to temper my actions?

A FATHER'S GRATITUDE

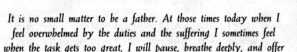

It is no small matter to be a father. At those times today when I feel overwhelmed by the duties and the suffering I sometimes feel when the task gets too great, I will pause, breathe deeply, and offer my gratitude for the opportunity to open my heart.

There are days when it takes all you've got just to keep up with the losers.

—ROBERT ORPEN

Lighten up today. Go back to bed. Go buy some marmalade and real butter and crusty bread. Make toast and have some tea. Read a mystery writer to whose level you swore you would never drop. Lie on the grass and watch the clouds swirl. Nap. Chew some Juicy Fruit gum, mindfully. Read a magazine you got at the checkout counter. Read it in the bathroom.

Give up. You'll never catch up in any case.

Religion points to that area of human experience where in one way or another man comes upon mystery as summons to pilgrimage.
—FREDERICK BUECHNER

The narrow focus of pilgrimage can lead us to a life of deeper understanding and greater delight, as fathers and as sons of fathers. If we can pay close enough attention to the present moment, looking away from past and present, there is sufficient mystery to continually remind us that the path is constantly right underfoot. Did you watch your child as she was born? Do you feel, in reflection, the deep sense of connection with the natural world? Does the sun startle your senses each day and the moon bring quiet and awe at night? If there is not enough mystery, right here and now, to point to the pilgrimage not that you are summoned to, but that you are already on, you must look more deeply. The mystery is all around. Examine the ground beneath your feet. There is the mystery, the summons, and the path of pilgrimage.

I live in mystery.

> *The sad truth is that most evil is done by people who never made up their minds to be either good or evil.*
>
> —HANNAH ARENDT

I have been haunted for years by the image of a mole, blindly pushing its way through soil, roots, shale, and sand, noticing nothing, responding only to its needs. While this is an accurate description of a mole and nothing extraordinary, the persistence of it in my thoughts/dreams and the aversion it always brought to me made me understand it was worth understanding.

Through circumstances I came to see that this was my way of seeing evil being done out of an indifference to choosing between good and evil. Pure selfishness and self-centeredness will always lead to inadvertent evil. Like this: *Whoever has the most toys when he dies, wins.* Let's not be fooled. How many of us feel that way? Isn't the satisfaction of material needs, no matter how grotesque or harmful, primary for most of us? If we choose to lead a good life, to live the finest way we know how, would that still be possible? If we reflected on the consequences of our choices, how many would we not make at all?

Have I chosen a path?

Listen or thy tongue will keep thee deaf.
—NATIVE AMERICAN SAYING

One phrase in the liturgy of the Tiep Hien order of Vietnamese Zen Buddhism is the vow to "listen deeply to hear what is said and what is left unsaid." This is not possible without putting ego completely aside. I cannot listen to you if I am chattering away with judgments about this or that, considering my replies, or preparing to either defend myself or protect you. It takes practice to listen this way. It challenges our notions of fixing and helping and our concept of ourselves, the father, as The One Who Knows.

It is not possible to know without listening.

The butterfly counts not months but moments,
And has time enough.

—RABINDRANATH TAGORE

When I was living, for a month, at Plum Village, a Buddhist retreat center in France, I would often take long walks through the countryside on free afternoons. On one such hot and lazy afternoon, I stopped by a field of beautiful wild grasses, punctuated by low shrubs and patches of tall sunflowers.

My attention was caught by two small white butterflies who rushed and soared among the grasses. I lost myself in them for a while, following their moves, imagining nothing, assuming nothing, considering nothing, hoping nothing.

In a blink, they were gone. I walked on, more slowly. The grass shimmered about me. A thunderhead capped a hill in the distance. The rain came that night, as I lay in my tent.

Pay attention!

Take my advice—I'm not using it.

—ANONYMOUS

Advising, helping, fixing, particularly, but not only, when unsolicited, are invasive and injurious. The message is that I am more and you are less; I am whole, you are incomplete; I know, you don't. With our children and our family and friends, I suggest that we consider *service* rather than advising, helping, or fixing. When I serve my son, I am bringing my wholeness to his wholeness. I am honoring him rather than dishonoring him. I am saying to him that I am offering all of myself to him, in celebration of his wholeness.

Take my wholeness, I can't use it up alone.

A FATHER'S GRATITUDE

This place where I live may not be everything I wished for. I must remember today, when I feel that what I have is not enough, that I have everything I need for today. I will express my gratitude for what I have.

The glory of God is in man fully alive.
　　　　　　　—SAINT IRENAEUS

We are fully alive when we are awake in the present moment. It is only when we are fully engaged with the world that our "aliveness happens." This is so because we contain this greater world. We are a part of it, not apart from it, in our true selves. Observing the sunflower fully expands us to our true dimension; brushing the baby's hair with mindfulness expands us; being lost in lovemaking expands us; surrendering to love expands us to contain the entire universe.

The fully compassionate person is fully alive.

Religion, as a mere sentiment, is to me a dream and a mockery.

—JOHN HENRY NEWMAN

Sentimentalized religion is the religion for those who have lost touch with spirit. It is not merely an empty religion, but an insidiously dangerous one, for it does not require intimacy but only form and the small mind. True religion dances the life of the religious one, opening the big mind to the gods and spirits who are its ancestors and its progeny. The religious life is joyous and demanding in equal measure.

I am a practicing Episcopalian Buddhist; my wife is, I would say, an intuitive Gnostic; my stepchildren practice the Jewish faith in their father's home and join me in Buddhist practice at our home, with sporadic forays into my grounding as an Episcopalian. Our son Willie is a Buddhist today, or maybe a Christian today and a Buddhist tomorrow. What is important is that I see in our family a spirited desire to know the transcendent, and a deep and wonderful understanding of that which connects us all.

My religion reveals my connectedness and my aliveness.

A DAY OF MINDFULNESS

This is a day of retreat and renewal. Please see Appendix A.

Convictions are more dangerous enemies of truth than lies.

—FRIEDRICH NIETZSCHE

I have had the great good fortune to have ongoing relationships with three great spiritual teachers for a number of years. They are Zen Master Thich Nhat Hanh, Abbot John Daido Loori, and the Very Reverend James Park Morton. I have noticed one quality they share. When I am with any one of them, in a one-on-one situation, their attention is totally on me. I get the sense that they come to me free of assumptions, prejudices, and most especially, convictions. They are present and, in a remarkable way, empty. There is nothing there. No Thing. As a result, I leave these encounters, even the most difficult ones, knowing that I have been fully heard and fully understood.

I try to do that with my children and with all those with whom I come in contact. It is a bitch. I am so bound up in convictions that I sometimes fear I serve my children not at all. I began this practice when Willie was born, in 1989, and have improved only a little bit. I hope, to steal a phrase from Father Thomas Merton, that "the desire to please [them] is in fact pleasing."

Can I be open to my children, without convictions, when they need me?

Men go forth to wonder at the height of mountains, the huge waves of the sea, the broad flow of river, the extent of the ocean, the course of the stars—and forget to wonder at themselves.

—SAINT AUGUSTINE

I have a friend, Kathy Fusho Nolan, who is a Zen monastic, a medical ethicist, and a pediatrician. We once were talking about the Buddhist statement "How wonderful, all beings perfect and complete, lacking nothing." Fusho said that in her work as a pediatrician, she would often have to talk with new parents whose newborns did not somehow meet their expectations. In some cases the sorrow would be rational: a child born disfigured in some way perhaps. In others, the unhappiness might be from lesser "faults." She would tell them, from a compassion I know to be endless, to consider how remarkable it is to be born a human being, to take this holy form.

Another friend sometimes disciplines himself to think of people as just "cells dividing," on and on and on. Such a wonderful idea. "My, aren't his cells dividing in an *interesting* way?" we might say about Richard Gere, for example.

It is a wonderful thing, to be born human.

I was not looking now at an unusual flower arrangement. I was seeing what Adam had seen on the morning of his creation—the miracle, moment by moment, of naked existence.

—ALDOUS HUXLEY

Here is a story my wife told me. A friend of hers had a new baby, just six weeks old at the time of this incident, and an older daughter, age about six. One evening the friend and her husband were sitting in the kitchen, talking. Hearing conversation in the background, they stopped and listened and realized that what they were hearing was the voice of the older child, carried by the intercom from the infant's room. Their daughter was saying to the baby, "Please tell me what God is like. I'm starting to forget."

Our experience of reality leads us away from the realization of God, but it will also lead us back. Living fully in the present moment is a kind of ongoing resurrection. We are endlessly incarnated right here, right now.

"Please tell me what God is like. I'm starting to forget."

Don't limit a child to your own learning, for he was born in another time.

—RABBINICAL SAYING

For decades, parents have been saying that kids have it rougher than they did when they were kids. Now they are right, even having been sentimental or off the beat before. It is harder to be a kid. My daughter, born in 1964, and my son, born in 1989, were born in different times. We have "improved" life so irresponsibly in Western culture that it is nearly unlivable. We are winging along in the midst of a ubiquitous and seductive technological culture that threatens to overwhelm us at every turn. We are so caught up in the gadgets and the costly corollaries of spiritual materialism or romanticized "return to nature" schemes that the centers have dropped out of our lives.

It ain't gonna go away! We can't ignore it, bomb it, or criticize it out of existence. It, this technological culture, contains too much good. What the spirited father needs to do is to keep it in perspective for the kids, and the truth is, the old perspectives don't work.

What is your perspective on the times of your children?

All you under the heaven! Regard heaven as your father, earth as your mother, and all things as your brothers and sisters.

—SHINTO SAYING

What if, for just this one day, you could keep this idea of family in mind? What divisions that you imagine would crumble? What hostility would cease? What war would end? What desire would be extinguished?

What if, for just this one day, you could keep this kind of humility working for you? Sky; father? Earth; mother? All things; brothers and sisters? Would you feel lost?

Would you experience intimacy?

Today I will see my place on the larger map.

A FATHER'S GRATITUDE

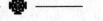

I am grateful to be on this earth, at this time, with these people. It is a time of magic and tragedy and I am grateful to be present for both.

*He who rejects change is the architect of decay. The
only institution which rejects progress is the cemetery.*
                                    —HAROLD WILSON

"If it was good enough for me, twenty years ago,
it's good enough for you." "If it ain't broke, don't
fix it."

I'm not you, twenty years ago.

It's broke.

The unit of survival is "we," not "me." That is
a new and frightening idea, but the old one, the
materialistic one that says that man is master of his
fate and captain of his soul, has failed. I don't think
that we need to worry about the endurance of what
is eternal, but to care for our children, we need to
look more deeply at our refusal to accept the enormous changes in the way the eternal expresses itself.

It's broke. Let's fix it.

Bread for myself is a material question: bread for my neighbor is a spiritual question.
    —JACQUES MARITAIN

In my family, we bake bread to take to homeless shelters. We are not alone in this at all and claim no merit for doing so. The point is that all of us contribute in some way to the daily bread of others. Our work and time are tied up in that bread. Baking it is not an isolated event, perceived only tangentially, as a day of lectures or tepid practice of denial might be. This is realy bread, fragrant and delicious, and often flawed, which is made by people for people.

Consider that loaf of bread. Get lost in the metaphor. In Zen they say " . . . seventy-four labors brought us this food. We should consider how it comes to us." Here we have the opportunity to be the source of the bread, baked and delivered. This is an opportunity for gratitude for the flour, the heat, the water, the yeast, and the time that lives in this bread we bake.

Consider the bread you bake today.

A FATHER'S SERVICE

There is a child somewhere nearby who needs my help. I will put everything on hold today—clear my calendar, cancel my appointments, take the day off from the ordinary—to help that extraordinary child, even if she never knows. I will learn to be "inconvenienced."

There, but for the grace of God, go I.
—SOURCE UNKNOWN TO AUTHOR

Consider this statement. It says that I am chosen; I am different; I am better than and apart from the object of my (secret) scorn. This is a way of thinking that carries only ruin. It protects us from feeling the suffering that pervades the whole universe. It protects us from feeling the suffering. It protects us from feeling. It diminishes our aliveness and makes our path mean and short.

Whitman said, "I contain multitudes." In times of isolation and separation from self, "other," God, and the Earth, we need to look deeply at who we really are. Do we "contain multitudes"? That is, do we see that we are not so much our brother's keeper as we contain our brothers? My brother, Phil, and I are blessedly close. When he is in pain, I feel it, and vice versa. Our father's lingering illness, so pitiful to see, has hurt us both and brought us closer, in our mutual suffering. Phil and I could not possibly look at Dad and say, "There, but for the Grace of God, go I." What we can say, I offer to you today.

There go I.

God, whose love and joy
are present everywhere,
can't come to visit you
unless you aren't there.
—ANGELUS SILESIUS

I am made up of many not-me elements. This is one of the clearest teachings of my teacher Thich Nhat Hanh. In me, my ancestors live. I look at the palm of my hand and see my great-uncle Lacey McDaniel and my ancestor Mahakasyapa. There also is "the negro boy Jim," as he is identified on a bill of sale, dated 1855, and signed by my great-great-grandfather.

I was a flower and a cloud and may well be such again. Grass will grow from my forehead and birds will carry my blood on their migrations. I am fire and smoke, grass and dust. I dwell, unknowing, in God.

What is this self I'm so certain about?

A DAY OF MINDFULNESS

This is a day of retreat and renewal. Please see Appendix A.

> *Man can become part of God's unity, which is eternal, only by forgetfulness of self.*
> —RABBI NACHMAN OF BRATISLAVA

It is difficult, at first glance, to feel comfortable with the idea of no-self or with the proposition of being self-forgetting. Reasonably so. We might think, "If I forget myself, what happens? Do I disappear, is my personality annihilated, do I become just like everyone else? Isn't this idea of no-self nihilistic and dreary?"

To find the answer to these questions, we only need to take a look around. Look at those who have served most selflessly. They are not ciphers. They are women and men of great power and serenity. When we look closely enough, we see the immensity of their bodies, minds, and spirits. The tradition of self-forgetting is in the groundwater of all the great mystical and religious traditions.

If we look closely enough, we see that it is the selfish ones whose "personalities" are limited and mean, and whose lives are nihilistic and dreary.

What is this self I'm afraid might disappear?

Ignorance is the curse of God.
                    —WILLIAM SHAKESPEARE

We need to ask what it is to be ignorant. If I am ignorant of physics or of poetry, I might be missing a great deal of pleasure, but I do not believe that this means I am God-cursed. I know very little about mathematics and I can't find Sumatra on a map without some diligent work. But this is not ignorance; it is not a curse.

What can I possibly be ignorant of that would cause me to be cursed by God? That is, how can I be so unworthy as to be cast out of the intimacy of God's presence?

Just that! Not to know the intimacy of God's presence. Not to know that God breathes in me, deeply and completely, is to be cursed and alone.

What breathes me?

> *The sky and the strong wind*
> *have moved the spirit inside me*
> *till I am carried away*
> *trembling with joy.*
> —UVAVNUK

What is spirit that it can merge so completely with sky and strong wind and can cause joyful trembling? We talk of the spiritual life of . . . men, women, fathers, mothers, children, all sentient beings. Is this thing Spirit different for each or the same? Does it live in some physical spot or is it merely an idea, all dressed up in fancy, to keep the demons at bay on the dark ride?

Is this spirit separate, enmeshed, immanent, or distant? Can we "attain" the spiritual, like climbing a mountain, or do we discover it by sitting still?

Is spirit created or is it eternal, unborn and undying? Is it emptiness or is it the largest container?

Spirit?

Spirit shines in the dance of the birds outside my window, the curve of the trees in the wind, and the sound of frogs greeting dark. It lurks in pine, deer scat, oak, and humus formed of winter snow and maple leaf. It shines without my intervention. It shines only without my intervention. When I say deer scat, oak, and pine, there is only some shit and dried leaves.

When the mind is still, spirit shines.

We buy gear and go to Everest and overwhelm the mountain with technology, and when we get to the top we haven't challenged ourselves. We haven't changed. We're still just assholes.

—YVON CHOUINARD

Like many, I spend some time each year on so-called retreat. "So-called" because these retreats are anything but. I consider them, instead, to be enterings into the real stuff of my life. The days of retreat are spent in simplicity; there are few distractions—no talking, no eye contact, no diversions. Just sitting or walking purposefully, with breaks for work, sleep, and very formal silent meals.

I am presented with a range of Everests at each retreat. I often fail to make it even to base camp. But the less equipment I carry, the more likely I am to make it partway at least and maybe get a few glimpses of the snow leopard or the ox. It's when I try to get away from it all by taking it all with me that I am so encumbered that I can't move an inch.

When I head for those mountains with a fresh mind, I have a chance of seeing them. When I take a conditioned mind along, I am deaf, dumb, and blind.

How do I climb my mountains?

> *Our children are growing up now in an ethically polluted nation where substance is being sacrificed daily for shadow.*
> —MARIAN WRIGHT EDELMAN

Doesn't that irritate you? What Marian Wright Edelman is saying here is too true to allow the luxury of contemplation or musing. Right this moment, the shadow is stealing your children's life away. I wouldn't worry much about the moral irresponsibility or mystical uselessness of anger. Anger is a perfectly appropriate response to the dread induced by this vast material and technological culture, run by the greed-heads and served by those of "passionate intensity" who daily run the lives of children into charnal ground and who cleverly offer up both sickness and cure. You know what I'm talking about.

There is no time for anything but action. With our children pointing the way, we can see the substance and begin to live it. Robert Coles has said that he has seen "the heart of the Bible" through the eyes of children of eight, nine, and ten. Look with the children. The shadow is cast by the tall ones, dominating the landscape. Look with the children who can still see past the shadow.

What sacrifice can be made to end this sacrifice?

And the young ones?
In the coffins.
—MIQUEL HERNANDEZ

I want my son and daughter to be untouched by war. I want Willie never to be a military man, bleak and dreary in popinjay uniform with cheap brass dull gleaming. I want Kam not to serve and not to see the one she loves the most in a closed coffin with some flag on it, an honor from a grateful country, grateful that another has died in another's place.

These are naive desires. I know that even if my son and daughter don't see war, yours might, or his. I don't want that either, but it is going to happen. We're going to keep killing the kids and we're going to keep glorifying the soldiers.

I want to mourn and honor the soldiers, my kids and yours. I want to end the ways of war, but I never will. Look around. Thanatos reigns. Can you see it any differently? If you do, you are naive. We all do our time, although I wouldn't have expected to, a Tennessee farm boy under blue skies smelling of dust and honeysuckle. How naive. "The sky's the limit." That's what my friend, Lieutenant Rodriquez, believed too, and so did the sons who buried him under that sky.

Don't think you are going to put the coffin makers out of business.

> *For me, the word "warrior" and all the martial images need to be stopped. I don't want to renovate or spiritualize them . . . They are degrading metaphors, the ones that damaged us.*
>
> —SAM KEEN

The images that come to my mind when I hear "warrior" have nothing to do with peaceful or spiritual beings. Sticking such words, willy-nilly, onto a word that is associated with WAR is a futile exercise. It has been argued that certain peaceful behavior has requirements, such that identifying the obstacle, planning actions, and following through relentlessly with total commitment *is the way of the warrior.* Isn't that also the way of the peacemaker, the healer, and the prophet? Isn't it also the way of the madman, the zealot, and the sociopath?

Please, find another word; or get unstuck from the metaphor; or just get to work without having to give yourself a title. Consider the images that come to mind when you describe yourself as a warrior. Don't look at what you see when you figure it out or justify it, but just at what comes up. Are you alone? Embattled? Relentless? Unforgiving? Is there a little grandiosity? Consider as well how the metaphor has damaged you.

Isn't there some work that isn't War?

Against Stupidity, even the Gods struggle in vain.
                                    —SCHILLER

When my friend Debbie sent me this quote, I disliked it. It struck me as mean-spirited and fatalistic. As I sat with it for a while longer, I found myself liking it for reasons I was not entirely happy with; it has an elitist and morally superior ring. There lives in me an elitist and an egalitarian, and I think that both are bogus. My most wholehearted and ego-free reaction to this quote is simply yes, this is probably so. Stupidity causes great problems in this bloody world. There are stupid people. That is, there are people who are blinded by prejudice, self-righteousness and pigheaded "-isms" of remarkable variety.

When I looked this deeply at this small thought and could expand its significance far enough, I saw that I myself was prejudiced: against speaking ill, even when ill so desperately needs to be spoken. Looking even more deeply, I saw that the definition of stupidity included me.

I must struggle against my own Stupidity.

A FATHER'S SERVICE

There is a place in my neighborhood, perhaps the street itself, that is not good for the children. Today I will begin the effort to change that.

If a vain man meets a holy man, he will envy only the respect that others show him.

—HARI DASS BABA

The holy men have a hard time of it in our culture. The charismatic, the clever, and the slick get along nicely, thank you, but the truly holy are viewed, by many, with suspicion and anger. Consider the monks who immolated themselves to protest the war in Vietnam. Some laughed at them; some criticized them; some hated them. And some respected them. It was difficult to do. I couldn't. I was a soldier then, a warrior if you please, preparing to fight in that very war, and what these men and women were saying with their burning flesh was too hard for me to hear. I saw them on the evening news or saw their pictures in the newsmagazines and would not yield to that holy part of me that saw the deep love and sacrifice in their actions. I saw only the attention they were getting and I did not like it. Their love made what I was doing, with rifles and bayonets, profoundly wrong, and like so many young warriors, I could not stand to be wrong. So I derided these gentle monks. That derision contaminated my soul. My heart would have none of it.

Years later, I became a member of the Buddhist community that they began. Over time, my hatred of them was transformed to understanding and deep respect. The answer to my question "What the hell are they doing?" blew in the wind for a long time. It finally came to rest when my mind began to be free.

Transformation is a reality. We only need to be awake to notice it. We see it best in our personal stories.

Among all nations there should be vast temples raised where people might worship Silence and listen to it, for it is the voice of God.

—JEROME K. JEROME

Noise seems absolute and unmoving. There is the exterior noise, which may be orderly, the radio always on, or chaotic, what sounds like gunfire and explosions on city streets. Airplanes fly overhead, whining their importance, while the television provides a noisy simulacrum of what's real. There is our interior noise. The steady gab as we judge, position, consider, and order the subvocal murmur of ancient fears.

We create noise to keep the wolves at bay, like fires in the night. When we begin to practice silence, we befriend the wolves, and our souls learn to gambol in the deeper forests. This silence is the vast and finally unknowable whisper of the world spirit. The totality of it evades us eternally, but we can begin to listen for it. If we could just shut up.

Shut up.

> *Disneyland is a white pioneer's idea of what*
> *America is. Wacky American animals. American*
> *conviviality, zappy, zany, congenial and nice, like*
> *a parade of demented, bright Shriners.*
> —JONATHAN MILLER

I took Willie to Disneyland when he was four. We had a great time and it cost a horrid amount of money. I was a vegetarian when we arrived at Disneyland, but by the time we left, only thirty-six hours later, I had eaten two enormous cheeseburgers. There was something so darkly corrupt about the place that I turned savage to survive. I probably should have spun back on ole Minnie Mouse and wolfed her right down, with a little Heinz 57 and a cold Budweiser. Willie snuck around behind her and lifted her skirt to get a peek.

These parks and palaces are pretty dark places. None of us, on our deathbed, is likely to say, "I wish I had made one more trip to mickeyworld." Think about it. Which desires come up in amusements parks? What fears? Look at Goofy without your blinders on and he's one scary son of a bitch. What itch gets scratched at squirrelworld?

What drives my need to be amused?

A FATHER'S SERVICE

---◈---

Today I will spend one hour working in a facility I know where children are cared for.

In the current family-hurting culture, families must do two things to survive: They must protect themselves from what is most hurtful to the health of the family and they must connect with what is good outside the family.

—MARY PIPHER

This interlude of several days will be spent looking at Dr. Pipher's wonderful notion. The work of fathers is so urgent and her idea so strangely revolutionary that we're going to hang out with it for a while.

Dr. Pipher says that the current culture is family-hurting. How are *our* families hurt? The question cannot be answered usefully. How is *my* family hurt? How is *your* family hurt? Those questions can be answered in useful ways. We need to look more deeply at the dangers in order to deal with them strategically. It might be that we all face some of the same dangers, but not all of them, and dealing with the specifics is what's going to get us healthy.

My family is hurt by living in a specific suburban township where consumerism is a family sport and a truly spiritual life is considered "sick." My family is hurt by a school that makes a big show about doing something about the drug problem on campus, but does nothing. My family is hurt by not knowing our neighbors, and by not wanting to.

Overall, all our families are hurt by isolation, but what, in the culture, hurts **your** family?

What harms the children harms the family.

The children are not safe until they have a community that cares about them. That community is not *all* of some institution, like a school. It might be part of that institution: the math teacher who cares about the kid who can do Rubik's Cube faster than the gods; the coach who takes the girls and boys on the soccer team for cocoa and talk after every game. But to just turn them over to the school misses the mark considerably. The "school community" is a sales pitch, not a description of a useful reality.

Community includes me. Otherwise, I have only an institution, outside of myself.

What harms the children?
Violence on television!
No. What harms children is *violence*.

Let's not let the politicians get away with having their little hissy fits about Televised Violence where children see murder, when children ARE murdered, in their homes or on their streets, on a regular basis. Make no mistake. Shielding the children from televised violence misses the mark, again, if we don't shield them from the violence that is visited on them or their peers in the real, nasty, violent, and angry world they live in.

Representations of violence and violence are not the same. I cannot shield my family from only one.

Turn off the TV whenever there is violence. Good idea but way short of the mark.

Turn off violence whenever there is violence. This is where the protection starts.

If Mom and Dad punish, spank, yell, throw things, insult, or rule, there is the violence to turn off. If Mom comes home drunk or talks only about work or if Dad hides in his den, his lair, his male domain, there is some of the violence against the family. We need to look more closely at what harms the family. Often the family is one of the sources of harm. We need to be careful not to project the source of harm onto the larger culture and its things.

What hurts?

This problem is so vast, the outlook so grim, and failure so close at hand that we don't have the luxury of fixing the blame. Leave that to the national nannies and the politicians. Look to yourself. Look to your home. Look to your family. Look with the eyes of compassion, wide open, and search for the harm, forgiving the harmers. All the harmers. There is no single and simple sign of harmlessness. We'd like to think so. The popular culture offers promises of "instant long-lasting relief." If only . . . we returned to traditional family values. If only . . . we could move to the country. If only . . . there was a spiritual revival. If only . . . someone else would take care of it!

Someone else is not going to take care of it. Something else is not going to take care of it.

Joko Beck says the common cry is "I want, I want, I want, the world to be my parent." Our families live in the ways of harm while we hold this adolescent view. The world is not my parent. The schools are not my parent; the corporation is not my parent; the church, temple, mosque, synagogue, zendo—not parents. The world and its institutions have one requirement, rarely met, in order to join the flow of my life. They all require my active and selfish involvement.

I have met precious few people who have the quality of fearlessness I am describing here. Here's what I seek—fearlessness, openness, and a ferocious engagement when moral lines are crossed. If I can develop these, then the world of things and senses flows within me and without me, as the poet said. I suspect I will never develop them fully, but I offer them as goals, the North Star, for those who seek aliveness.

What is it in the culture that is "good," that our families can connect to? How do you make that determination?

In Buddhism they talk of the three poisons: greed, aversion, and delusion. Is that which you seek to connect to born of these poisons? Is your attraction to it based on these poisons?

A family afternoon at the mall is rich with all three. A family afternoon solving a jigsaw puzzle probably isn't. A family afternoon playing video games at home . . . There's a rough one. What about going to the movies? Storytelling? Going to a restaurant? Cooking a feast together? Going to The City? The Country? A Friend's?

Are places of worship and service touched with the poisons?

What is it to "connect" with that which is good in the culture?

Do we connect at the mall? With "amusement" parks? Theme anythings?

Only as slaves are connected to their work.

Here is a test of connection.

Can you breathe, consciously and calmly, in this place or situation?

Breathing in, I am here. Breathing out, I feel safe.

Breathing in, I am calm. Breathing out, I feel connected.

Breathing in, I know this is a good place. Breathing out, I share it with those I love.

Breathing in, I feel strong. Breathing out, I feel gentle.

Here is another test of connection.

Are you a part of this: this thing, this institution, the group, this event you think you are connected to?

Or is there a sense of "it" being done for you, requiring no imagination on your part?

Are you proud to be in this?

Or grateful?

A FATHER'S SERVICE

Every day I see children who do not have enough to eat. Today I will see that one of them gets fed. I can make a meal for a child who I know is hungry.

A DAY OF MINDFULNESS

This is a day of retreat and renewal. Please see Appendix A.

Ignorance is the curse of God.
  —WILLIAM SHAKESPEARE

So long as I see myself as separate from Other, I live in ignorance. It is not "there but for the grace of God go I," but "there go I." I may not be my brother's keeper, but I am, inextricably and forever, my brother's brother, and all my feelings of aversion to him injure me.

What father, other than an ignorant one, could mock his own child? Only the ignorant father, for example, isolated by his delusion of separation, could see his child suffer, and turn his back, smiling and bowing to the "authorities" to whom he gives the care of his child.

But . . .

Ignorance is not corrupt or bad or evil. It simply is and could not exist without the existence of enlightenment and compassion. Ignorance is, simply, our usual condition, and it can be transformed!

Wake Up!

While all complain of our ignorance and error, everyone exempts himself.

—JOHN GLANVILLE

I am not exempt. I was in my late forties before I saw the connecting fibers. I still struggle to remember them.

And you? Exempt?

An ounce of parent is worth a pound of the clergy.
—SPANISH PROVERB

As a father, I cannot afford to judge my child by your rules or standards. That is putting my child, all the children, at some place Other than where they and I truly are. In fact, I should endeavor not to judge my children at all, but when I must try to see them clearly, my eyes are the trustworthy and loving judge.

It is not the job of the church, the mosque, the temple, the sangha, or, I must say, the village to parent my child. All of those are important and I must solicit them, but when they judge harshly or when their judgments are based on values I do not share, I must be harsh myself and let my child know that he is safe and worthy and lovable.

How can I let the child know that she is safe and worthy and lovable?

Am I?

A FATHER'S SERVICE

There is a playground or park near where I live. Today I will go there, alone, and strike up a conversation with another father. I'll let him know what a good job he's doing.

Don't make your will before dying for an ideal: make a kid who will be worthy of his father.
    —GRAFFITO FROM THE FRENCH STUDENT
                                    REVOLT, 1968

If Willie is to be worthy of me, then that worthiness must never become a consideration for him. Nonetheless, I would hope to leave a kind and courageous son rather than a basement full of cash or a wasted land outside my tiny green plot.

Who needs to be worthy of whom?

The end of all is death, and man's life passeth away suddenly as a shadow.

—THOMAS À KEMPIS

Thich Nhat Hanh once asked, in a lecture hall, "What's the hurry? It all ends at a funeral." This statement from this gentle Vietnamese monk, who has seen such suffering in the world and who has done so much to relieve it, had a powerful effect on me. I saw clearly for a moment how I hurried from place to place, thought to thought, action to action, and I saw clearly as well how much I was missing. There is no imperative to "see it all"; indeed, it can't all be seen. There is, however, the opportunity to see what is right in front of me fully and intimately. And if I see suffering, to relieve it, and if I see joy, to encourage it. No hurry.

It is no mean thing to be born human. Why waste it in pursuit of what you've already got?

As favor and riches forsake a man, we discover in him the foolishness they concealed, and which no one perceived before.

—LA BRUYÈRE

No one is more deceived by the vain and foolish man than the man himself. What do you think your children think of you? They are not, yet, so vain themselves or so deluded that your vanity and ignorance are invisible to them. They forgive you for it, but they also wish you would come out of hiding, before it's too late.

What will be left, when not much is left?

INTERLUDE:
Stepfathers

I have been a stepfather for a quarter century at this writing. At this writing, my oldest stepchild is in her early thirties, and my youngest is eleven. There are three more in between those two. There were two fathers, and mothers, involved in creating this mob. I married the mothers, and stayed married to one of them.

Being a stepfather is a bitch!

For the next few days we are going to take an interlude for stepfathers. If your children are with a stepfather, as one of mine was for many years, please come along.

We'll start by saying what we only say in anger and private. Being a stepfather is like using a condom. It just ain't juicy enough. Here's the other thing we think about a lot. Why doesn't HE do his part? Why can't we say those things, evenly and gently, from our hearts?

Because we never found the right people to say them to. It's time to get a group together, isn't it?

INTERLUDE:
Stepfathers

If the movie *The Stepfather* is one of your favorite movies, you are not alone. You are also pretty healthy. When the "villain" stops in the middle of a phone call and says, "Wait, who am I here?" it is not too difficult to identify, is it? His subsequent actions are certainly extreme, but no one among us is without the occasional murderous urge. We step-dads need to acknowledge, to each other, that we have ugly feelings about this situation from time to time. I am both a father and stepfather, and I can assure you that they are different. As a father, I feel an intimacy with my children that I do not feel with the stepkids. It's a tricky line to walk, but easier when I step out of the delusion of "loving them as if they were my own." I don't. Can't. I do not mean I don't love them. I do love them very much, but it feels different from the love I feel for my own two children.

INTERLUDE:
Stepfathers

Most stepfathers I know aren't happy with the relationship between their wife and her "ex" (if only he were, we say). It doesn't matter if she detests him, is afraid of him, cares for him, or, the worst perhaps, hides from him with their children. He is still in her life and always will be. And the children are his, no matter what we might like to pretend to the contrary.

What about this relationship between your wife and her former husband and the father of her children?

How do you deal with this? Write to me about it.

INTERLUDE:
Stepfathers

———————

At one time, I was so twisted around by the way my wife and the former hubby did their particular dance that it occasionally threatened our marriage. I would argue, try to fix, pray, ignore, "let it go," shout, and do everything I knew to get it to change. It didn't change. Here is what I realized. At last.

It has nothing to do with me!

INTERLUDE:
Stepfathers

If you had stepfathering to do all over again, what would you do differently?

I'm offering this one as an opportunity for those of us who have been doing it for a while to correct course a bit, and for those just jumping into the boat to start off with some guidance from the bloodied.

I would stay out of the power struggle with the children for my wife's attention. I would lose that one, agreeing with her that we would come together each day, away from the kids, when their very real needs for reassurance had been satisfied. I would assure her that I was not one of the children and would endeavor to act that way.

I would create a daily ritual for alone time with my wife. Coffee together in the morning, every morning, with special cups in a special place. No planning of the day or talk of children allowed.

INTERLUDE:
Stepfathers

If you had stepfathering to do all over again, what would you do differently?

I would be an uncle, not a father. Being an uncle allows me to relax the rules, cut out the power plays, and knock a hole in the mask of authority. Uncles let the kids have ice cream for breakfast. Uncles are listened to without an overlay of suspicion and fear. Uncles attract affection, wide-eyed and awe-filled, and give it back in full measure. Uncles are outsiders, kinda, and invite the kids to the wider worlds that they come from and where they live and have such interesting adventures.

Uncles can see you fail and not take it personally.

I think I might be an uncle if I had fathering to do all over again, too.

If you had stepfathering to do all over again, what would you do differently?

I wouldn't take myself so seriously.

A FATHER'S SERVICE

Today I'll clear out my kids' closets and, together, we'll donate the old clothes to a shelter where we know they will go to other children.

When a man prays, do you know what he's doing? / What? / He's saying to himself: "Keep calm. Everything's all right; it's all right."

—UGO BETTI

Prayer has an uncertain reputation. For some, it is an enforced and senseless ritual; for others, a daily childhood reminder of the ongoing threat of death while sleeping; and for yet others, the open and joyous offering of our total beings to the deep mystery of vast emptiness.

When we pray, from our hearts rather than merely a prayer book, our spirit returns to us and to the truth of the present moment. Everything, in fact, is all right; right there where we kneel, humbly, or sit, or stand, arms raised toward infinite and everlasting space.

The family that prays together *is* together, right then, and the future and past are suspended and revealed as irksome phantoms, incorporeal and unthreatening. The family is calmed. That prayer, the family prayer, is not led by anyone. It is the true communion of the soul of the family with the deeper life it senses around it.

How does the family pray?

INTERLUDE:
Clarity and Anger

A matter that becomes clear ceases to concern us.
— FRIEDRICH NIETZSCHE

In order to see clearly, the "I" must be closed. So long as my filters of need, aversion, opinion, and dishonesty are operating, I cannot see what is right before me. I am not able to be intimate with an object of derision. I cannot understand the pain of a child or the sorrow of my partner when all I see is refracted through the crusted mirror of my own vanity and foolishness.

It is when I stand apart from suffering that I cannot have clarity about it. The suffering is an impenetrable miasma, formless and threatening. If, however, I throw myself into the suffering itself, I think I will suffer all the more. I will. This is inevitable.

You can't drain the swamp without getting wet.

INTERLUDE:
Clarity and Anger

Thich Nhat Hanh teaches that suffering is not enough. When I throw myself into the suffering of another, I am not merely joining in the suffering, I am providing the way out. As an ex-junkie, I know, marrow-deep, the suffering of addicts. And I know the way to the end of suffering. What is important to me is to never forget the suffering, because if I do, I will finally start to fake the way out. "I" will get in the way. My ideas, prejudices, aversions, and long-lived twist toward self-righteousness will close the gate.

Does this mean I can have some clarity only about such matters as have affected me directly? What is the way to the boundless compassion of the bodhisattvas, the saints; the self-forgetting love of a great rabbi or the all-seeing clarity of a lama?

INTERLUDE:
Clarity and Anger

The Dalai Lama states forcefully that "compassion is not a feeling. It is a reality." The way to that reality is by seeing clearly. We need to evoke, in ourselves, the spirit of Manjushri, the Bodhisattva of Great Understanding. How do we do this thing?

When I went for my morning walk this morning, I was very angry about a situation in which I felt I had been wronged. I hurt and it was a hurt that summoned older hurts I thought I had laid to rest years ago. I began my walk, blaming one particular person for the pain I felt. As I walked, the endorphins started to churn, my body warmed, and "I" shut up, in the bliss of early morning mountain light and air.

Walking along a back road, I remembered my own advice. In thinking of Other, in this case the person who hurt me so, I need to think, "There go I." At that moment I could see it was not the situation that was hurting me, or the person, but my idea about both. My hurting idea was that I was separate from the person and the situation.

INTERLUDE:
Clarity and Anger

————————

When we can begin to see ourselves in every situation of suffering, we can begin to see the end of suffering. When the understanding of "self" includes rather than excludes, our hearts open and we act. There is clarity and the reality of compassion. It is a fragile thing.

It is my experience that nothing so effectively destroys clarity as does anger.

INTERLUDE:
Clarity and Anger

Nothing on earth consumes a man more quickly than the passion of resentment.
—FRIEDRICH NIETZSCHE

At the moment that anger begins to arise, we have the best opportunity to conquer it, and the best opportunity to encourage its exquisite burning.

Being angry brings a sense of royal power, invincible and potent. Manly. When I am angry I am unapproachable. There is me and there is everything else. At no point do I feel more powerful and never am I more alone.

Alexander Yelchaninov calls anger "Black Grace." In that blackness I am living in total illusion. I feel powerful and am impotent. I feel invincible and am weak.

When that white heat is burning in my gut, I am not only useless in stopping what I would stop, but am actively participating in feeding its power.

INTERLUDE:
Clarity and Anger

_____

Anger provides immediate gratification in an impatient culture. We have become accustomed to getting what we think we want.

Entertainment? Push a button. Information? Surf the net or read the news. Sex? Right away. Satisfaction is guaranteed. Quick, Easy, Guaranteed Relief. Pain? Take these. Sorrow? Take those. A plane explodes in midair? Keep watching the TV news until it's all fantasy; pixels lighting another Movie of the Week.

Pissed off? Blow up.

Entertainment fails, information never fills, sexual pleasure fades, and you have to take aspirin or Prozac again.

Blow up? Breakdown.

INTERLUDE:
Clarity and Anger

Pissed off? Wake up!

It's no longer useful to work so hard at explaining anger. We need to leave the discussions to those who have less to do than most of us. There is too much pain and suffering and too little time for us to have to read another book or see another TV special or spend another five hundred dollars to let another ballroom guru tell us why we're angry. The weight is more or less equal on our shoulders, and the bad guys are just as close to you as they are to me.

Don't you think it's time to do something? Short-term quick stop and long-term cure?

INTERLUDE:
Clarity and Anger

I had had enough of getting angry when I lost it while driving (familiar?) during the holidays (that, too?) in a mall parking lot. (At least my parents weren't with me—one less arrow in the quiver.) Some fellow disapproved of my driving and showed his displeasure with a familiar hand signal and an even more familiar, if physically impossible, for me at least, sexual suggestion. I saluted him back and made several similar suggestions to his rapidly re-treating bumper.

A minute or two later I had to pull over to the side and get control of my breathing, blood pressure, and general physical demeanor. I realized that this was more than I could take. Willie was just six and I didn't want him to spend the rest of his childhood with Daddy dead from a heart attack in his early fifties.

That was the beginning of the end of free-range hostility.

Short term? Consider self-preservation.

INTERLUDE:
Clarity and Anger

————————

That same night of mall madness, I drove on, with a few changes. I had been listening to a Rolling Stones CD, *Sticky Fingers*, in the car. I turned it off. I left my double espresso sitting in the cup caddy, untouched, and tossed my double-fudge chocolate brownie in the trash. I didn't need that much of that kind of fire in *my* belly, thank you.

Six months later saw the end of sugar, white flour, and caffeine abuse. A clever friend of mine once said that a whole host of our emotional problems can be solved by a cheeseburger. Changing my diet has made enormous differences.

(As it happened, I had eaten my last "cheeseburger in paradise," St. John in the U.S. Virgin Islands, that is, the previous summer, but I know what my friend means.)

Turn down the heat in your blood, bud.

INTERLUDE:
Clarity and Anger

That same night I called some close friends and told them what had happened. How I had scared myself and was going to sit quietly with this problem of anger, the expression of anger, in me, by me, until I felt comfortable with it. Witnesses.

I'm still not comfortable with it, but as it has begun to fade, I have been blessed with clarity. The lessening of anger has been not only replaced by clarity but cured by it. Light expands. Darkness recedes. The Black Grace yields to light.

A FATHER'S SERVICE

Today I will pick up a magazine that is devoted to children. If I find an article I really like, I will write a letter to the editor and thank him or her for it.

A DAY OF MINDFULNESS

This is a day of retreat and renewal. Please see Appendix A.

Kabir says: Student, tell me, what is God?
He is the breath inside the breath.

—KABIR

The Zen practitioner sits, still and silent, following her breath. The infant's breath is sweet with milk. The sad old man, slumped in worn trousers, next to you on the rush-hour subway, sighs his day's defeat into his chest. The winded sprinter, triumphant, gulps in breaths of stadium air and breathes out, slowly.

If you are looking for God, just see the breath. There is nowhere to go. God breathes in you and about you. Look closely.

Sit with a sleeping child and watch him breathe. Address God directly, right then, by saying, "Sweet dreams. I love you."

My God, my breath.

INTERLUDE:
On the Ordinary

When the mind is at peace,
the world, too, is at peace.
Nothing real, nothing absent.
Not holding on to reality,
not getting stuck in the void,
you are neither holy nor wise, just
an ordinary fellow who has completed his work.
—LAYMAN P'ANG

INTERLUDE:
On the Ordinary

On this desk at the cabin in the Adirondacks, there is a cobalt blue glass, filled with sweetened iced tea. There is a telephone, gray, with buttons and lists.

There is a letter, unanswered, from Nancy Samalin, a turquoise stick pen, and a newsprint program from a traveling Shakespeare troupe, with autographs from Dylan Trowbridge (Tybalt) and Holly Lewis (Luka) in a spirited production of *Romeo and Juliet.*

There are three windows just in front of me, each with fifteen panes, peeling white paint, and pull-down shades. Flap, flap, flap. A small butterfly jerks about in the orderly branches of one of a pair of fir trees.

There is a small framed postcard portrait of a crazy wanderer, carrying a bamboo walking stick, with a frog seated squarely on his head.

I spoke with Willie last night. He lost another lower tooth. He whistled his news to me.

INTERLUDE:
On the Ordinary

A friend once said, "We need an altar on every street corner." I suggest that just by looking more closely at the ordinary objects, on every street corner if you wish, we will see that we are surrounded by altars.

An altar, in any religious tradition, is a place of transformation. While we are doing our ordinary stuff, we have the opportunity, at every moment, to transform our experience of that ordinary stuff. We are able to return to our original nature, our true selves, by simply returning to the present moment.

We have all had the experience of arriving at some destination with no recollection of the journey. As we begin to transform the ordinary, we see that every moment is an arrival.

INTERLUDE:
On the Ordinary

The ordinary is transformed to the sacred. That is half of the alchemy. The other is that the sacred is transformed to the ordinary. The ordinary contains the sacred. The sacred contains the ordinary. They co-arise.

My ordinary cup of morning coffee, viewed deeply, contains the spirit of many people who have helped to bring it to me. When I look closely at that cup and that coffee, I can feel awe and humility. In Zen they ask, in liturgy, whether their lives and practice "deserve it." Imagine drinking your skim latte grande with that attitude!

Willie's curved neck, with its light sprinkle of fine blond hairs, in shadow while he sleeps, is sacred to me. When he was younger, I saw that little neck as a miracle. Today I see it, as well, as a perfectly ordinary neck. Ordinary in that it is one of millions of little necks with glimmer of hair on a sleeping child. How miraculous that such a thing is ordinary. How precious and worth standing up for.

When I can see that the sacred and the ordinary are not different, then I am beginning to see truly.

INTERLUDE:
On the Ordinary

There is a story that my father has told me that I will pass along to Willie in a few years. It's a simple enough tale, about my grandfather, a small-town doctor in west Tennessee, and a horse and buggy, and a sun-dappled summer afternoon.

It's not a sentimental story, nor is it a heroic one. No lives are saved, no treacherous journeys are taken, no morals are offered. There is not one special effect in the story. No exploding cars, no threatening aliens, and no guns. Everything is plain. My father told me the story without doing anything more than telling it. He was a wonderful speaker, but no actor. It is just about something that happened one day when he was a boy.

It is such an ordinary story that it has stayed with me for over forty years.

Can you recall an ordinary story you have heard? Something real that happened to someone you love? Can you pass it along to your children in an ordinary way?

What is an ordinary story from your life that needs to be passed along, just for its simple ordinariness?

*Look lovingly on some object. Do not go on to
another object. Here, in the middle of this object—
the blessing.*
—FROM *CENTERING*—TRANSCRIBED BY PAUL REPS

When I first became a formal student of Zen, I
went through some initial tests or barriers, including
an all-day sit, an official petition of the teacher to
become his student and more. At the end of the all-
day sit, from dawn to dusk in early July, the four
of us who had completed the task went to the home
of our teacher for an informal tea and to present
him with simple gifts as a part of our larger ritual.
I had chosen a small vase, about six inches high and
perhaps three inches in diameter. It was beautifully
glazed; a deliciously funky piece.

At the appropriate time, I touched it to my forehead, to indicate intimacy, and handed it to the
teacher. He took it, touched it to his forehead, and
said, without another glance at the vase, "Oh, are
you a potter?" Before I could tell him that I was an
unemployed actor, his attendant took the vase away
from him, peremptorily, I'd say, and said, "What a
wonderful vase. Feel how heavy it is."

That attendant was a great teacher at that moment, for me and, I suspect, for my formal teacher.

One thing at a time, fully seen, blesses deeply.

A FATHER'S SERVICE

Today I will skip lunch entirely. I will take the money I would have spent on lunch and I will give it to someone I don't know who needs it.

> *For us, each working day begins with the dream-shattering blast of the alarm clock and a heavy dose of caffeine, the better to clear our heads for the busy demands of the "real" world.*
>
> —THEODORE ROSZAK

Is there some other way to wake up in the morning? Can you find a way to move gently from sleep to waking, carrying with you the important fragments of dreams you made?

Here's one. Sleep until you awaken. Go to bed early enough and undrugged enough to actually get the sleep you'll need. Then get up, have the caffeine if you must, but sit quietly with it. Look at the cup. Savor the flavor. Consider how this cup and this coffee made it to you this morning.

What is the reason you have already given that this is a stupid idea, this getting up after a full night's sleep without an alarm clock? Look at it closely.

Why is there no time to enjoy a cup of coffee? Why must it have extra caffeine?

Who runs my sleeping? Who sets my clock?

I have just three things to teach:
simplicity, patience, compassion.
—LAO-TZE

Meditate on these three words today. What are they in the "real" world? Where do you find them? How are they related, if at all?

What are they in your life?

Simplicity. Patience. Compassion.

There is a crack in everything God has made.
—RALPH WALDO EMERSON

Leonard Cohen says the crack in everything is where the light gets in.

Consider what is imperfect in your life—cracked, unfinished, a burr in your saddle. That's where the good stuff is. I know a man who has a perfect home. No cracks. His own children say that it's as if no one lives there. As fathers, we need to encourage idiosyncrasies. We need to applaud the strikes, those ungainly and awkward swings at a decidedly wayward ball. "Sweet liberty, what a terrible cut that was, darlin'!"

At more beautiful levels, we need to applaud the rebel. True teachers will tell you that the "good students" always do the same work and that they, these few true teachers, feel their spirits expand when the kid in the black fat jeans, with the sullen hopeful grin, turns in a scribbled Blakean masterpiece in three lines.

Look for the cracks. Seek the light.

What a man knows at fifty that he did not know at twenty is for the most part incommunicable.
—ADLAI STEVENSON

Wisdom is the shadow of anger. Where one is, the other lurks, often unacknowledged. In my youth I was, for the most part, angry. Today I hear about the anger of men; about the genesis, expression, and power of it.

I wish I heard more about, or saw more evidence of, the shadow.

Forgive who you need to forgive; acknowledge your debts, including the very great debts to those you have hated; see what needs to be done; and stand up.

What I know at (more than) fifty is communicated easily—by my actions. My actions are my only possessions. Anger imprisons the benedictions I offer; wisdom impels them.

What is it that wisdom and anger share? How are they shadows of each other?

If called by a panther,
don't anther.
—OGDEN NASH

If there is no room in our lives for silliness, then we are getting overly crowded. What is so important that every day must contain gravity, endurance, and forbearance?

Can't you just giggle and play the day away?

Don't anther!

For a Future to be Possible
—TITLE OF BOOK BY ZEN MASTER THICH
NHAT HANH

It's no longer safe to "get around to" seeing what needs to be done. There just isn't time to hesitate. We have to stand up now. Action powered by compassion makes a future possible. Action powered by self-interest or anger is too fragile. Action powered by compassion is the strongest tool in the box and the one we must use.

We can look closely, today, at what imperils the future. To do so, look at what imperils the children. Most of us need look no further than our living room, or kitchen, or garage.

One action, powered by the fact of compassion, is all we need do today. If we fail to take that one action, the failure is geometric in its repercussion, but merely arithmetic when taken.

What is the one action, powered by compassion, to take today to make a future possible?

Poets aren't very useful,
Because they aren't consumeful or very produceful.
—OGDEN NASH

Kathleen Norris claims that monks and poets are the most degenerate members of society. They point out the cracks where the light gets in. They model lives of inquiry, quiet, and spirit-consciousness in a mall democracy. Beware the poets and the monks. They live deeply rather than merely long. They are the idiosyncrats amongst the bureaucrats.

Have you read a poem lately? Do you feel, as so many fathers do, that you would, secretly, like to spend a weekend in a monastery? Or on retreat? Do the churches you pass linger in your mind? Do you come to after a period of time lost, staring at the salt shaker you hold poised above the scrambled eggs?

Listen. The poets whisper simple songs to your still heart.

Look. The monks are gesturing "Pssst, come here, be loved."

Stop.

A FATHER'S SERVICE

I will clean my children's rooms today.

Around us, life bursts forth with miracles—a glass of water, a ray of sunshine, a leaf, a caterpillar, a flower, laughter, raindrops.

—THICH NHAT HANH

When we live asleep we miss the miracles that are provided, willy-nilly, at all points. There is no plan to this profusion of miracles. There is no evidence of intent that we can be aware of. The whole cosmos commits random acts of kindness, if you please.

Waking up is such a simple thing. There is no demand except from our hearts, often unheard, and no work to do except to learn to breathe.

For today, do just this: notice **that** you breathe! Don't count the breath, manipulate the breath, wonder about the breath, none of it. Just notice that you breathe. When you catch yourself at it, simply say something like, "Hmmm, breathing."

My breath, my life.

The best mirror is an old friend.

—TRADITIONAL

After a gap of thirty-five years, I got back in touch with my best friend from adolescent times. We were instantly back in the rapport we had felt all those years before. There was no getting reacquainted, only facts to be caught up on. His name is Carlton. Carlton and I were together as friends from age eleven to age sixteen—a fecund time.

In a time of change and movement, when, like me, so many kids will live in many different homes in the course of their early years, we must consider the need for friendship. And make room for it.

Do my children have friends like I had?

*Leopards breaking in—upon whatever our compla-
cencies—is the nature of religion.*
                                        —LINDA SEXSON

A small hard sun, diminished by mist and brilliant
red, rose over Lake Champlain this morning. I had
gotten up early to meditate as usual, seeking more
understanding of a koan, a riddle, impenetrable by
ordinary logic, that my teacher assigned me two so
long years ago. I was going about my usual business,
the little rituals of getting ready to sit, such as lighting incense, touching it to forehead, putting on old
worn robe, fretting about my *rakusu*, the little repre-
sentation of the Buddha's robe worn by Zennists,
when a sidelong glance out the attic window caught
that sun, that leopard.

The *rakusu* is still in the case that Dairyo made
for it, the robe is lying on the bed. I had to come
downstairs to my writing table to tell you about that
sun and the mist on the lake. Just as I opened the
door to my porch, a flock of inland gulls took off
from the field out back.

Stay alert. The leopards are everywhere.

By thoughtfulness, by restraint and self-control, the wise man may make for himself an island which no flood can overwhelm.

—*THE DHAMMAPADA*

Wisdom is anger's shadow. The energy of anger, bleak and consuming, transformed, becomes the scalpel that slices away ignorance and selfishness. Anger says, "I am alone and omnipotent." Wisdom says, "I am connected and powerful."

Some say that the anger that men have felt is justified. I do not think this is very helpful. If we feed the seeds of anger, we stay angry. I suggest that we begin to feed the seeds of wisdom. The children need wise fathers, not angry ones, no matter how "justified" the anger.

Today I will water the seeds of wisdom.

A FATHER'S SERVICE

Today I will make a list of all those persons who are involved in helping me raise my children. I will call the ones I speak to least and thank them for all they have done.

A Father's Responsibility

The children and their children will inhabit this earth long after I am gone. I am responsible for the condition of the earth. Today I will consider how best to exercise that responsibility.

A DAY OF MINDFULNESS

This is a day of retreat and renewal. Please see Appendix A.

You are part of the infinite. This is your nature.
Hence you are your brother's keeper.
—SWAMI VIVEKANANDA

U_s and *them* is where the trouble starts. We get into clubs, men's groups, fraternities, neighborhoods, twelve-step programs, sanghas, or congregations and throw up walls that say we're a little different over here. No offense, but we aren't like you. Then we huddle together and protect our imagined uniqueness.

Try this. When you see someone you think is different from you, really different, imagine that person really is your brother or sister. Look at him or her and consider that you grew up together, played together, fought with each other, and never made up—until later, anyway. See that person, and that one over there, too, as part of you.

She is, you know.

There go I.

> Zen works miracles by overhauling the whole system of one's inner life and opening up a world hitherto entirely undreamt of. This may be called a resurrection.
>
> —D. T. SUZUKI

When the worst storm is over, all that's left is the foundation.

In Zen practice, we strive for wisdom, compassion, and insight. The cliché says that we break down in order to break through. In the ordinary course of one's life, events will inevitably occur that lead, practice-free, to the potential for the same. The foundation determines whether we are born again.

I believe that my greatest understanding came not because of divine intervention, but because I had a bedrock that prepared me for it. Karma, if you wish. When I look at Willie and the other children who look to me, I try to consider the foundation I am helping them build. I am not interested in preparing them for careers, or to be useful and productive or even to be happy. I am interested in seeing them develop strength of character and deep internal resources.

What foundation am I helping the children to build?

> *The perfect Way is without difficulty*
> *Save that it avoids picking and choosing.*
> *Only when you stop liking and disliking*
> *Will all be clearly understood.*
>
> —SENG TS'AN

This and that. Them and us. Right and wrong. War and peace. We live in the world of all of this. The world of this and that is all about us. When Thich Nhat Hanh was told that his hermitage at Plum Village might be closed by the local authorities, he said that he could always find some other place.

Today, when Pauline called to tell me that there was a hitch in the selling of our house, I looked for someone to blame. There were plenty of candidates, of course, but Pauline told me to stop it, there was no one to blame.

I didn't know what to do. I'm writing this in our cabin in the Adirondacks, a place of many places to go mountain-biking, and that's what I did. An hour into it, I had exhausted the list of enemies. I wish it hadn't taken so long. But I understood. The house will sell to the current buyer or it will not. My feelings about it are irrelevant.

My ideas about my life aren't my life.

Man, desiring no longer to be the image of God, becomes the image of the machine.
—NIKOLAY BERDYAYEV

The family has become pathologized, first, and mechanized, second. Community has become virtual.

Don't be fooled. Your family has greater depth than any ballroom guru or academic researcher will ever see. Each member of it moves her own way, in and out, dancing and sitting this one out. There is one person in your family who is, well, different. Different only. When you see that, you will begin to see him.

Virtual means "in effect," not "really" or "realer." It is a chimera. Stay away from virtual community until there is a stink and a pathos to it. Play on the net and go home to the community of stories, with depth and awe and holiness. Just like your family.

The machine is not the enemy of family and community. But it's cute and cuddly. Beware.

Whose Family Values?

. . . in family life, be completely present.
                                        —TAO-TE-CHING

Consider how simple it is to be a runaway father, sitting at the dinner table. As a society we are justifiably upset about the dads who leave their children or who are kept away from their children. If you are with yours, then look at how present you are.

A father who tells rather than listens and then turns away when the tear forms in the child's eye is running away. When a child asks for help and is given an attitude rather than an answer, the child is, at that moment, unfathered.

We need to understand that mere physical presence is not enough.

To be fully present is a challenge. We are surrounded by distractions, some very real, some bullshit, that carry us away. We are also—admit it—afraid of the consequences of intimacy, of being fully present in the life of our children.

In the present moment, there is nothing to fear. The children need us there.

Things derive their being and nature by mutual dependence and are nothing in themselves.

—NAGARJUNA

The tree outside my window has no separate existence. That tree contains rainstorms, sunshine, birds, squirrels, and fallen leaves, for starters. That tree contains the beat of the wing of an exotic bird, long dead, in a Southeast Asian forest. It contains the work of those who worked this land and it contains the bodies of soldiers who froze on this very ground in the war for independence.

My father is dead. He lives on in me. I can find him by looking deeply and I can talk to him. My great-uncle Lacey is long dead, and when I am on my horse, charging down the meadow, Uncle Lacey is riding right behind me, checking my boots in the stirrups.

Father, uncle, tree, bird, fallen leaves, sunshine, and rain clouds. What miracles!

A FATHER'S RESPONSIBILITY

My children learn how to deal with lovers and friends from the way that I deal with lovers and friends. I am responsible for the way they will relate to others in the future.

You can only find truth with logic if you have already found truth without it.
—G. K. CHESTERTON

We know how to be with our children. Our intuition will always tell us what to do. The sadness is that we have forgotten how to listen to that intuitive self. It is not so hard to relearn it. In every situation wherein we are called upon to serve the children, we can practice quieting the mind, perhaps through following the breath or saying some sacred syllable or prayer. Count to ten.

Then listen. The answer that is about the child, not about you, is the answer. Through patient practice of this technique, we will learn to know and trust the voice of intuition. Then, if we wish, we can build theories around it, but right now the time is too short and the children are suffering.

Listen!

> *Children, one earthly Thing*
> *truly experienced, even once,*
> *is enough for a lifetime.*
> —RAINER RILKE

The rock song advises us to *teach* our children well. I say that we need to *show* them well. This little book is full of suggestions on developing the power of mindfulness. This is not a power to be taken lightly. Develop it and let the children see you use it. As you learn to look, with your entire body and mind, at just one true thing, to look until you and that thing are indistinguishable, your children will see true aliveness in you. And just as they do what you do, no matter what you do, they will endeavor to learn it. Your legacy will be profound.

I will learn to show my children aliveness.

Look around. My sweet Jesus, what is going on around here? What's that sound? Look, there's a flash of light just yonder, next to that hidden green holly bush, popping little red ornaments. Whoa, there is some tricky stuff going on out of range of the shimmering circle of TV night light, and drone of music unheard all day long. It gets real interesting when you've got your ass in the wind and your ears up. Doesn't it?

Look out!

God is in me or
else is not at all.
—WALLACE STEVENS

Where do you want to point when you point at God? Careful now, the kids are watching very closely. Is She Up There? In the dog's eyes? At The Sharper Image? Surfing the net? A myth, fairy tale, or metaphor . . . for other people? Do you explain Her to your children or tell them what other people believe?

Carl Jung said he didn't believe in God, but that he knew God. Angelus Silesius said God can't come to visit you unless you aren't there. Zen Master Dogen said that to study the self is to forget the self.

Where's God.

"But the emperor has nothing on at all," cried the little child.

—HANS CHRISTIAN ANDERSEN

My wife anchors me, and the whole family, when the winds of fashion threaten. The good this does for our children is inestimable. Here's one small example. The school our older boys go to has been sucked into the "dress-down Friday" vacuum so beloved by corporate executives. There are even some days, such as "weird day," when the poor kids are encouraged to dress, well, weird. Our boys see through it, although one of them did take a little coaching, and just don't bother.

The emperor is never more naked than when he dresses as he is permitted to dress, no matter whether it's shamans' robes or three-piece suits, if he doesn't see the "must" in "may."

Yeah, the parable goes deeper, but let's start with fashion's eyewash.

What are you wearing today?

A FATHER'S RESPONSIBILITY

Today I acknowledge that I have responsibilities to my children that no one else should be allowed to perform for me. By exercising my full responsibilities today, I am teaching my children about the future that will not include me.

In facing our own deep-seated need for security and belonging, can we see the immense attachment and dependency on groups and organizations?
—TONI PACKER

Widen the circle. We do great damage to ourselves by holding on to the group, the party, the program, the nation, the community, to define and keep secure our mechanisms for dealing with suffering. One of the saddest examples of this is those twelve-step groups who take upon themselves a unique suffering and a unique end to suffering. "They just don't understand." How sad! We are saying that others don't suffer the way we do, or that others don't see the relief of suffering the way we do. Just so are political parties who invite you out the door if you don't believe as they do.

This behavior, this dividing into tribes, causes suffering. It does not relieve it, it causes it. If we teach our children that our tribe has it right and the other guy's tribe has it wrong, we are setting up a fight, within and without, that'll twist them for years.

Ask again: what other? Widen the circle.

We do not see things as they are. We see them as we are.

—THE TALMUD

We live in a culture that pathologizes and simplifies out of aversion to uncertainty. We are eager to name any behavior that deviates from an increasingly narrow norm, pathologize it, that is, in order to keep the sufferer at arm's distance.

When a child is troubled, we need to learn to say troubl*ing*. The problem is our response to this child, not the child herself. The heart of every child, of every one of us, is the same. It is so very difficult to see that. I want to be angry about this, but I am only looking at my own failures. The finger points at me. A troubling child in my life has been my greatest challenge. I have not done it well. If you are like me, take heart. I've gotten better at it. If you are not, and have taken a troubling child into your heart, write and tell me how you did it.

Look deeply at the child; and yourself.

Don't seek reality, just put an end to opinions.
                                        —SENG TS'AN

It is my opinion of things that causes all the trouble.

This kid is not like those kids, so this kid needs help. Those people don't think the way I think, the right way, so they should change. Then everything will be OK. There is a God; there isn't a God. Tourette's syndrome is caused by Agent Orange. I shouldn't have drunk so much. My wife is crazy and my in-laws are schizy. All snowboarders are thugs. Lobotomize Republicans: It's The Law.

Right and wrong. Right or wrong. Right. Wrong.

Hush your mind!

O to be delivered from the rational into the realm of pure song . . .
                                      —THEODORE ROETHKE

Here's how to write a kind of poem title. Make three columns: *a, b, c,* if you wish. In *a* and *b,* put adjectives or other modifiers. In *c,* put nouns. Take one from column *a,* one from column *b,* and one from column *c.* That is the title of your poem—like "Drunken Chocolate Pagodas."

Today I will sing a bunch of poems.

The fundamental delusion of humanity is that I am here and you are out there.

—YASUTANI ROSHI

To begin the practice of intimacy, listen to what the children are saying and what they are not saying. If you listen closely enough, you will hear your own long-ago voice coming back to you. It is not so difficult to understand the fears and joys of a child when we make even the barest beginning of listening deeply. To listen deeply means that you must get out of the way.

There is no room for the child to express herself if you keep the room crowded with your own needs and ideas. For this practice of intimacy, gently dismiss your ideas and listen. When your ideas come back, notice them and dismiss them.

Begin this practice today and continue it for ninety days. Then it will be yours.

Only plain things have real taste.
                                    —ANONYMOUS

Eat a carrot today. Or an apple or a radish. Take a while. Do this in a quiet and private place. As you eat consider how this food came to you. Who else and what else are involved in sustaining you today? Consider your good fortune in having this food, this time, this private quiet place. Consider how to express your gratitude.

Taste completely.

Abandoning things is superior, pursuing them is inferior.

—YEN T'OU

For a week or so, I considered getting myself a particular very expensive sports car. A silver one, classically styled, basically unchanged in over twenty years. An investment in classic and conservative elegance. Smooth, powerful, with a gut-rumble sound. Faster than greased owl crap too, by the way. You can imagine how much time I spent thinking about that car. I pictured myself picking Willie up at school in it or driving it, top down, into the city. What a man! I hadn't even bought it and it already owned me.

I got over it, but it wasn't easy. I sat with the idea and saw how having the damned thing would add to my dis-ease. I also saw that the pleasure such a car gave me was easily attained. If I saw one on the street, I could admire the line, the power, and the speed, and be done with it.

How many men do you know who are happy with their toys?

A FATHER'S RESPONSIBILITY

There are many businesses that harm children with their products. I only have to read the newspaper today to see what they are. It is my responsibility to see that just one of those businesses is shut down or reformed!

The path is long, the way uncertain. Bring sandwiches and a magazine.

—AUTHOR UNKNOWN

Lighten up a bit. It is terribly dangerous to take this "spirited" business much too seriously. When you get rid of attachment to toys, to people, to affiliations, and have only your spirituality left, your burden is far too heavy.

Let go.

Everything intercepts us from ourselves.
—RALPH WALDO EMERSON

Fathers need to practice poverty in order for our children to realize value. When the children have to struggle too often past all our things, our attitudes, our endless needs, to get to the heart they need, they will be defeated. If we aren't there, unencumbered, we lose ourselves and then the children are lost.

What is so important that we can't show up, open and empty, for our children? Is it such a fearful prospect, to see ourselves, that we are willing to sacrifice our children to those fears?

Empty out!

Today the future occupation of all moppets is to be skilled consumers.

—DAVID REISMAN

Consumers! Is it in your best interest to teach your child to be a consumer, skillful or not, first and foremost, at all? Do you want your beloved child to grow up to be a Consumer . . . with a Lifestyle? Do you say that you want them to be able to consume wisely? That is still consuming.

Here is the problem, beyond the ugly semantic one, of Being a Consumer. Consuming only takes in. Nothing goes out after the purchase. We warehouse and when we have too much, we get bigger warehouses. Here's the other problem with Consuming. It is a serious business. Serious in that it is a private act performed publicly. Consumers consuming are no more likely to speak to each other, or even look each other in the eye, than men in a whorehouse, a very similar situation.

Take a look. How is your "moppet" being educated to be a consumer? Look deeply!

God be in my head, and in my understanding.
            —SAINT PATRICK

If God is to be in my head, then I need to give her room. So long as my attitudes and opinions are crowding the place, I cannot give my children what they need; I cannot offer them Fresh Mind.

Fresh Mind is just that mind of God, clear and open. The mind of compassion. When I offer Willie Fresh Mind, I am able to hear what he is saying and what he is not saying. He needs that room to play. The mind of attitude and opinions is a place of snakes. I don't need to let Willie go there. I need to see that it won't kill me to have Fresh Mind, but Willie will be deeply hurt if I don't.

Who is in my head?

Do your work, then step back. The only path to serenity.

—TAO-TE-CHING

Attachment to results of your work is harmful to your health. But why does Lao-tze say here that this is the "only" path to serenity? We know he was often a vague and tricky fellow, made all the more so by his various translators; but Only? I suggest that to stick with your work, after it's done, is to miss your entire life, happening right before your eyes. Fretting over that meeting, that teacher conference, that talk with your daughters, that encounter with that son of a bitch your wife used to be married to, or the results of the basketball play-off pour forgetfulness on the present moment, the only place where your life is happening. Look at that slant of sun on the tree across the way.

Breathe in. Breathe out.

Fools take to themselves the respect that is given to their office.

—AESOP

My father had a Ph.D., earned from Columbia University when he was quite young. He was a man of great accomplishment, a scholar and innovator in his field. His work has touched the lives of hundreds of thousands of children, and his books have been required reading in many universities for many years.

He never wanted to be called "Dr." Alexander, and if you asked him what he did, he would tell you he "worked at the university." Once upon a time, only two years before his death, I remarked to him on the latest honor accorded him by his profession, which I had found out about by reading the newspaper rather than from him. He turned my remark aside and said that he just wanted to be remembered as the father of his two sons.

What is your Title?

Can you deal with the most vital matters
by letting events take their course?
— TAO-TE-CHING

I wonder how many children have been wounded by those who are trying to protect them from wounds. Look at the ardent work of those who set up programs to keep the kids busy. The children are too busy to make mistakes, to dream, to fantasize, to get into delicious trouble. We clip their wings and wonder why they can't fly.

It's for their own good, we tell each other, or we talk about how the world is a more dangerous place than it was. It is. But it is more dangerous yet if we deny the reality of it. And we deprive the future of the rebels who would challenge the King.

Can I learn to stay out of the way.

A FATHER'S RESPONSIBILITY

When I am hateful or greedy, I am teaching hate and greed. When I am kind and generous, I teach kindness and generosity. Today I will consider those ways in which I am hateful and greedy and I will begin the process of change. I vow with all beings to put an end to hate and greed.

We grow weary of those things [and perhaps soon-est] which we most desire.

—SAMUEL BUTLER

Some years back, I was struggling up a street in San Francisco, walking toward my apartment build-ing on California Street. I was carrying a garment bag with a couple of suits, a so-called carry-on bag, a briefcase, and a paper bag with a six-pack of Bud, a bottle of brandy, and some potato chips. Dinner. It was a hot, lousy day. I was desperately hungover and fatigued. About halfway up the street, I stopped and hollered, "I've got too much stuff."

That was a moment of deep insight. I knew, at that moment, that I meant more than luggage and "groceries." I meant despair, responsibilities, attach-ments, fears, hard-held opinions and views. By the time I finished dinner, I had forgotten, but the am-nesia lasted only three more years.

When I get too much around me now, including mere things—shirts, shoes, and such—I know I'm feeling "stuffed." And stop.

Unload!

Do not wait for the last judgement, it takes place every day.

—ALBERT CAMUS

Take responsibility. Check out your actions. Have you forgiven the bad guys? Is there anyone hurting because of something you've done or failed to do? Anyone? Is the world a better place in some small way, thanks to you?

Atone. Let go. Rest easy. You did good.

Who are those who will eventually be damned? Oh, the others, the others, the others.

—ELBERT HUBBARD

Who do your children think "the others" are? Have you taught them your brand of prejudice? Look deeply. We may claim lack of prejudice, but we practice prejudice in every opinion we utter, every putdown, every self-righteous act. The religious wars of this century, fought by zealots or popinjays, are merely *you and me* writ large. The only way those wars are going to end is when you and I make peace in ourselves. Our children will inherit a world of war if we continue to teach them about the Other in all our subtle ways.

There is no Other.

The way is near, but men seek it afar.
—MENCIUS

The only path you can walk is the one right beneath your feet. When someone tells you what the path is, run in the other direction. When someone points you toward a path, don't mistake the pointing finger for the path. You may go in that direction if you wish, but the path you find will have to be your own.

Don't look in churches, temples, or mosques for someone to show you your way. Look right where you are. If where you are is a church, a temple, or a mosque, your way is still right beneath your feet. There is only one prayer to pray, only one song to be sung, only one way to be followed. And only you can find it. It's nearby. Shunryu Suzuki said, "The most important thing is to discover what is the most important thing."

When we surrender to the current of our own lives, we are in the Way.

Warning! Lack of clear thinking about the spiritual life is likely to land you in a murky swamp, in the company of muddled minds, surrounded by an obscure cloud of occult claims and false mysteries.
—SAM KEEN—CITING A PURELY IMAGINARY SIGN ON THE SLOPES OF MOUNT ANALOGUE.

For the sake of the children. Every entry in this book should begin with that phrase. Imagine, from here on out, that they do. So. For the sake of the children, know what you are saying when you are saying *spiritual.* Are you speaking of obedience or doubt? Faith or practice? Superstition or mystery? Corporation or community? Comfort or risk?

I have come to realize, for example, that my spiritual life is not a matter of faith. I wish it were that easy. My spiritual life is, rather, about practice. There is no place I go, other than everywhere I go, where I live my spiritual life. The people I hang out with are my community. All of them. Butcher, baker, candlestick maker.

The Buddha said to be a light unto yourself.

It's just a movie.
        —US (TO OUR CHILDREN WHEN WE ARE
                    HORRIFIED BY WHAT WE SEE)

Today, describe to yourself what was happening on the screen when you last said that to a child. Immerse yourself in the horror of it. A disemboweling. A head tumbling across the floor. A child being slapped. Machine guns. Bodies in flames. A child being ignored.

It's just real.

Very often the pleasure you seek is the source of your sorrow.

—THICH NHAT HANH

Pleasure is a by-product. True pleasure is that pleasure that comes from the gut out. Sorrowful pleasure is that pleasure that comes from desire. True pleasure is a surprise. Sorrowful pleasure is anticipated.

When I take my children hiking in the Adirondacks we are not seeking pleasure. We ring a bell, bow to the mountain, and ask its permission to enter. We do our best to hike mindfully. For the past few years even Willie, the youngest, has stopped asking, "How far to the peak?" If we get tired, we stop and drink cool water, and eat raisins and chocolate. On a hard pitch, we bitch. The fog surprises us, the spotlight sunbeams show us wonders. Underfoot, sloughed mountain skin crackles.

After the hike they eat dirty-water hot dogs at a stand set up just outside of Keene Valley by an enterprising local fellow. Drenched with brown mustard and grilled onions, washed down with iced tea, they are new every time.

Hot dog ambush!

A FATHER'S RESPONSIBILITY

My children's future is determined today. Everything I do today will have an effect on the distant future. I vow with all beings to prepare a future today that I want my children to live in tomorrow.

The farther you enter into the truth, the deeper it is.
—BANKEI

As you begin to enter the truth, the "I" diminishes. There is room for God. There is nothing between the seer and the seen. No room for opinion; no anger, no blame, no bias, no other, no nihilism.

This is not the hole in the doughnut. Maybe it is the Whole in the doughnut.

Make no mistake, the personality does not disappear. Rather, you, whole, become the vehicle for the truth.

Take the plunge.

I did all those bad things that create character.
                                        —GERRY SPENCE

I used to hang out in a bar in Florida that was a crucible for "bad" things. It was a delicious hothouse. It smelled of cheap beer, sex sweat, Lysol, and motorcycle exhaust from the corral out back. There was one killing there—the cops did it—and too many guns tucked into boots. It was a place of lawlessness, betrayal, and violence. It was never quiet, twenty-four hours a day. Rats ran just beneath the floorboards.

I've been in worse places and done far worse things than I did there, but you'll never read about them. I'm grateful that I had such a place. It pinpointed the worst in me.

*But listen. It is not doing these "bad" things that creates character. Character is what comes once you **stop**.*

as my eyes
search
the prairie
I feel the summer in the spring.
—AJIDEGJIG (CHIPPEWA)

Can we ever be still enough to sense the absolute codependency that we inhabit?

How will you teach your children that without that lodgepole pine, they would not have dinner? How can they learn to see the movement of seasons? (How can they learn to see the movement of seasons *without* the consumer prod pushing the buttons?) Who will teach your children to listen for winter, the time of going to the earth? How will they learn to watch for summer?

Who will teach them to listen without judgment, feel without opinions, see with such clear eyes that the seeing becomes the seen?

Can you talk with other fathers about this?

the woman absorbed, the woman under tyranny
the contemporary woman, the mocking woman
the artist dreaming inside her house.
                                        —ANNE WALDMAN

Who've you got living with you? Best pay attention. Best write a poem about her. Best learn to listen to every word she says. Without getting in your own way. Best look at her with fresh eyes, openhearted and wild, every morning and every night.

Best hush.

> *I don't really feel my poems are mine at all. I didn't create them out of nothing. I owe them to my relations with other people.*
>
> —ROBERT GRAVES

This is another speed bump. There are several throughout this book, and all have the same sinister purpose. Please write a poem today. Write one every day. Write one every week only. Write one when you don't want to write one about why you don't want to write one. Write a poem when it's poem-writing time or when it's time to sit quietly wherever you sit quietly.

Look at your child. There must be some little characteristic, some place on his body, some idea of his that you can write about. Please do so.

This is not productive work. It is not responsible.

Send me your poems. Let's do a book together. Send them to me at the address in the front of this book.

A friendship from which every day disappears be-
comes an allegory.

—JULES ROMAINS

At the age of fifty-four, I renewed a friendship
that had lain dormant for nearly forty years. This
man and I had been boys together. We had once
hand-sewn a tent and gone camping on an island
off Miami for a weekend. We were debating-team
partners who were never defeated. We sat about
after school, at his house usually, and talked it all
over.

I don't think either of us realized how much our
friendship had meant, its sounds, tastes, smells, and
perceptions, until we renewed it. Without the conti-
nuity of contact, it became merely an idea. When
we made contact again, as different as our lives were
and as changed as we both were by the mere pas-
sage of time, we connected at a depth and with a
longing that surprised us both, and with an immediate sense of how little our differences meant.

We will be in each other's lives, every day, from
now on.

What boy you loved has grown into a man out of your
presence? Can you find him?

> . . . *technology [is the] the knack of so arranging the world that we need not experience it.*
> —MAX FRISCH

In my office are a computer, a combination fax/copier/scanner, a television, a stereo, and a telephone. Outside my window are a half dozen pin oaks, two Japanese maples, four hundred-year-old spruces, boughs drooped to the ground, some scrub pines, and plots of exotic grasses.

I think I'll go take a walk outside.

And you?

There is a Buddhist vow to "save all sentient beings." When I first heard that one and subsequently began to chant it regularly, I did so through a constricted throat, without conviction. What was it that made me so special that I was going to go forth and "save" those who were—what?—not so enlightened as myself? Over time, I've come to see that by making that vow, I am reminded how imperfect I am and how like those "others" I am. Not different, but the same.

My aversion to that vow came not from the reality of the present moment, so humbling, but from a childhood of preachers who spoke down to me, the sinner, who cussed and hid a bottle of wine on the sacred grounds and who snuck away from church to make out with Grace. I was a sinner, made in the image of God.

God has hidden in the last place you'd look.

I am against sex ed in school because sex is more fun when it's dirty and sinful.

—FLORENCE KING

Take a closer look at the person responsible, in your children's school, for the classes or programs dealing with Sex. And Drugs. OK, and rock 'n' roll. Then think of the kind of person you would choose to do this teaching, if it absolutely had to be someone other than you. I'll take Dr. John (the Night Tripper) over Dr. Ruth in a cocaine minute, and I know for sure that no one in a uniform who has to use initials (DARE) to get the point across will ever get the point across.

Not Dr. Ruth. Not Dr. John. Me!

The past pours unceasingly into the future. What
are your plans for this afternoon?

Were it not for the presence of . . . the infinite shapes of the delightful human tadpole, the horizon would not wear so wide a grin.

—F. M. COLBY

We need to pay closer attention to those we stick out on the edges, beyond the margin. We need to see what the ones sitting quietly on the sidelines can tell us about our game. I have learned more from the unreasonable and chaotic ones than from the calm and the just. The Cambridge Ladies teach a quick lesson, to be sure, but the Ancient Mariner draws me in.

I suspect that this is a fault in me. I should probably pass the mariner by the next time I see him and head on up to Cambridge and listen very deeply. Maybe the neighbors with the carefully tended lawns are my greatest teachers.

Sisyphus rides the bus to work.

*The evil is not what they say about their cause,
but what they say about their opponents.*
    —ROBERT KENNEDY (ON EXTREMISTS)

What do our children learn when they see and
hear us degrade, or condemn, or condemn in God's
name and on her behalf, another person? For example, I do not agree with the philosophy of *The Promise Keepers*. They frighten me. I dislike their beliefs
and their methods. However, I once rather publicly
condemned the men themselves. That was wrong
and I regret it.

Each of us has a tender heart, tinged with sadness,
as Pema Chodron so elegantly expresses it. Who am
I to condemn your humanity because you express
yourself in ways I do not agree with? It is very
difficult to be willing to see the tender heart in those
whom we disagree with. And nothing is more useful
than to discern that timid pulse.

Can I learn to listen more deeply to those I spurn?

A FATHER'S RESPONSIBILITY

———— ✖ ————

The earth is a fragile place. I will not harm it.

Most people repent their sins by thanking God they ain't so wicked as their neighbors.
—JOSH BILLINGS

When we judge another as unworthy, as less than ourselves, we are simply firing another worthy teacher. When that son of a bitch who voted for the wrong candidate comes into the hall and we shun him, we are diminishing ourselves. And when we greet him with open arms, bearing hidden daggers, dipped in poison for his unprotected back, the children see our hypocrisy and the ignorance is broadcast.

Seeing my neighbor as myself has been the most difficult practice of my life. And it is not complete, not by a long shot. Daily I try to stop myself at the moment of aversion and to breathe in the disease of the other. It is difficult. There is a cost. That cost is great, but I have begun to see that the cost of aversion is much greater.

Can you turn aside your aversions?

Children need models, not critics.
—JOSEPH JOUBERT

When Willie was four, he told me, with timid strength, to please sit down, right here, on the floor to talk with him. From that time on, whenever we need to talk, that's where we go. It reduces me in more than size to sit there and talk with him. It reminds me of my own healing smallness in the face of things as they are. Because I meditate daily, seated on the floor, it helps me to open my heart and mind to him; to keep my wits about me.

After we talk, we can wrestle!

He that will have his son have a respect for him and his orders must have a great reverence for his son.
—JOHN LOCKE

How do we come to reverence for our children? The dictionary says that reverence is a feeling of profound awe and respect and often love.

Consider your child. Where he came from. Consider the endless changes and growth she is capable of. Consider how unlike you your child is. Then take yourself out of the consideration. Consider this child as a stranger. Don't "know" or understand this child at all. Look at this child with your whole being, outside of expectations, needs, desires, aversions, and fears. Look at this child with unknowing. Spend some time, perhaps unobserved, and watch this great being as it lives the days.

Can you look at your child, for a few moments each day, with reverence?

1

Today look at your child as a stranger. Consider what this child is all about. What is the child thinking there, this stranger? Why is she doing what she's doing?

2

Look at your child only with your eyes. Try not to know what you are seeing. Let the eyes do all the work, mind in neutral. When you start naming what you see, say simply and gently, "Naming," and go back to just looking.

3

Look at your child with your ears.

4

Look at your child with eyes of peace.

5

Look at your child with your father's eyes.

6

Look at your child with your child's eyes. See your child as your own child might have seen her. Look very closely with your mind turned off.

7

Look at your child with the eyes of God. Stay with this feeling. It is you.

8

Look at your child as he will be when he is your age.

9

Look at your child with eyes that reflect back who the child is to the child. Let your child see himself in your look.

10

Look at your child with your entire body and mind.

A FATHER'S RESPONSIBILITY

My children are indescribably dear. I will not barm them.

*My miraculous power and spiritual activity:
drawing water and carrying wood.*
—LAYMAN P'ANG

There are sufficient miracles and moments of grace in the ordinary stuff of our lives to occupy us fully, without the need to "expect" them. Sadly, we have forgotten the miracle of the child we carry or the sacredness of a blade of grass. We think the sacred and miraculous must be waited for, or encountered only in very special places. All places are very special. Every moment is awe-inspiring. There is no need to wait, as if the spiritual were earned and the miraculous a reward. To arrive at the spiritual and to see the miraculous, we only have to stop moving and looking. Just breathe, in and out. Just do your work. Just care for the children.

Celebrate the ordinary.

We sit together, the mountain and me,
until only the mountain remains.

—LI PO

Each day we need to find time to completely disappear. We need to find time to disappear so completely that we don't know where we are. This is not so difficult. The bookstore and library are full of books on how to "turn off your mind, relax, and float downstream."

Get to a place, every day, where you don't know who you are. This is not the stuff of mystics and hermits. You've done it by mistake time and again. Making love, watching a baby, listening to the Mass in B Minor, being a child. Do you remember?

Today I will remember a time when I forgot myself.

A FATHER'S RESPONSIBILITY

To teach peace, I must be peaceful. To teach love, I must be loving. To teach compassion, I must be compassionate. To teach simplicity, I must live simply. To teach patience, I must be patient.

Not "revelation"—tis—that waits,
But our unfurnished eyes.
        —EMILY DICKINSON

The point of taking this daily pause is to furnish our eyes. If you are reading this book, you have already realized that there is nothing to wait for.

What is more difficult is to remember that when you're caught in rush-hour traffic or when the meat loaf burns. Here is how to see that which has been revealed. Don't wait. Just breathe in and out. Slowly and deeply, three times. Look around with eyes of peace.

It is important to be conscious of this simple practice. Just breathe.

All has been revealed. Just look.

When the mind is at peace,
the world, too, is at peace.
—LAYMAN P'ANG

Years ago I learned a prayer that I didn't like much. In it I was to ask that such and such a person, whom I was angry at or who I felt had hurt me, be given everything I wanted for myself and more. My kindergarten reaction was that I didn't want this person to have a Porsche, or to live in a grand house, or to find a wonderful partner or to be wildly successful.

Then I learned to look more deeply for what I wanted. When I discovered that what I really want for myself is a peaceful mind, a kind heart, and a generous spirit, I became completely willing for my worst enemy to have that and more.

If I want there to be peace, I must be peace.

My soul is as peaceful as a child,
sleeping in its mother's arms.

—PSALM 131

So long as I am poisoned with desire, hatred, and delusion, I cannot be at peace and my world cannot be at peace. Desire contains the seeds of compassion, hatred the seeds of wisdom, and delusion the seeds of awakening. I can choose, each day, which seeds I water. In choosing the facts of compassion, wisdom, and awakening, I liberate the entire universe and the child sleeps in peace.

I choose peace for my soul.

If in your heart you make
a manger for his birth
then God will once again
become a child on earth.
—ANGELUS SILESIUS

The peaceful center sits, covered with the cara-
pace of our defenses and fears. Our lives are filled
with perceived threats. That one over there is taking
advantage of me while this one close at hand is
going to get too close if I'm not careful. They will
get me if I let them, so I will stay closed. Only
those few whom I approve of can come in. Hey,
life's a bitch. You gotta take care of your own.

And all the time, God is breathing in us. The
challenge is for us to stop and listen to the breath
of God. There is no greater challenge.

Today I will wait silently for God.

*Tooting, howling, screeching, booming, crashing,
whistling, grinding, and trilling bolster his ego. His
anxiety subsides.*

—JEAN ARP

Silence evokes the spirits. In silence we hear the
deeper, more subtle sounds of life moving all about
us and within us. We strive to murder it.

What is it we get from all this noise? The illusion
of connection to power, I think. The noise, rush,
and imminence of our cities are like cocaine. We
talk about their energy when we mean their "rush."
These cities will stun you into an adrenaline high.
Has our anxiety gotten so great that we must kill
silence? (Is silence only a commodity? Do we consume silence? At the Silence Spa?)

If our children are young, they probably have
never experienced deep silence. We need to find the
silent places for them. We can start by finding our
own. They are as close as our hearts. Listen closely.

The children yearn for silence.

God is the friend of silence.
—MOTHER TERESA

We have befriended chaos and noise and have led our children smack into them. It is time to stop, to soften what surrounds us. The politicians and techno-mad educators would have us believe that connecting to the internet and the worldwide web are of value. There is no value in this for the children, already seeking to be narcotized by noise.

Can we begin to teach our children to connect to the inner-net? Can we let them learn the value of God's vast silence, more connecting to the source of reality than any computer net will ever be? If we have computers in our homes, we must have silent places as well.

We've got too damned many chat rooms and not enough quiet rooms. Is there a room in your house where your children can meet with God?

Hush.

*How can one better magnify the Almighty than by
sniggering with him at his little jokes, particularly
the poorer ones?*

—SAMUEL BECKETT

I have a friend who had a typewriter with a busted
e key. My friend is a writer and overly prone to
metaphor and hyperbole. The first time he discovered that the key was broken, he suffered a pathetic
epiphany. He decided, a priori, that God was telling
him to keep his *ego* in check; that his ego was broken. My friend rushed off to church, and then to a
coffee shop to share this great new understanding
with his friends.

It took him a week to get the typewriter fixed. It
took another week to understand that the point of
the broken key was that the key needed to be fixed.

The world is far richer in simple meanings than
great ones. God is found in your laughter and acceptance more often than in your ideas and aversion.

Laugh along. There's so little time for much else.

Our awareness of God is a syntax of the silence in which our souls mingle with the divine, in which the ineffable in us communes with the ineffable beyond us.

—ABRAHAM JOSHUA HERSCHEL

There is a spiritual breadth to each of us that far surpasses the meager reach of our minds and senses. It is subtle and, uncovered, it is immensely powerful. This lion awakes only in the silence of our communion with God. Awakened, he pads in serenity and courage and wisdom; an answered prayer in our very ordinary lives.

We hide behind our things and our ideas of things and fail to see the power of Things As They Are. It is that power that enlivens the lion, that is the lion. When we align ourselves with the Power of Things As They Are, we dwell in the sanctuary of God.

Without the practice of silence, we suffer in the noise.

I did not learn everything I need to know in kindergarten. No way.

Did you?

When you are real, you don't mind that it hurts.
—THE VELVETEEN RABBIT

It's our ideas about reality that make it hurt us so. When my father died, I was sad. I cried as I sat with him, both the last time I saw him alive, in a hospital room rich with the odors of an old sick man and his unguents, where he said, "Me, too" after I told him I loved him, and when I sat with his so pale corpse in a sterile funeral home viewing room. There was no an-aesthetic for me. My senses and heart were fully alive and I could see him so clearly.

Thank God.

A FATHER'S RESPONSIBILITY

*The work of this moment is all the work there is. I must throw my-
self into it fully. The work of this moment is all the work there
ever will be.*

*Chase after money and security
and your heart will never unclench.*
—TAO-TE-CHING

Do you know anyone who has gotten everything he ever wanted if all he ever wanted was money and security? No. That's kindergarten.

Do you know anyone who has not gotten what he wanted when what he wanted was peace of mind, a kind heart, and a gentle spirit? No. That's true maturity.

How's your heart?

Something is really wrong with us.

We murder, destroy, trample, rape, and starve each other at an unprecedented volume. This bloody century limps to a close with a list of atrocities too great to recite and too chilling to consider. If we're not on the front lines, we're hiding at the rear, behind gates and satellite disks. Our lives are on the line at every minute, and we don't even notice.

Don't look for good news here. Consider what brainless idiocy has been committed overnight in the name of God or Progress or The Greater Good. Then consider what you can do about it.

Something is really wrong with us.

Today I will pray as if my hair were on fire.

I was present at my son's birth. It was a difficult and scary one, but blessedly it didn't take so long, and Willie and Pauline were sound. I saw Willie emerge into the light, looking as if he had been in a bar brawl, and only moments later I held him. I carried him to Pauline and put him on her chest. I said something. I have no memory of what it was.

The moment I spoke, the feeling was diminished. The need to describe how I'm feeling rather than just feeling is not very useful. I suspect it's a way of staying safe. Safety is vastly overrated. Feeling with whole body and mind is a great gift, and I throw it away willy-nilly at the most sacred of moments. I wonder how much I have stolen from my children by telling them what they're up to rather than keeping silent and letting them know on their own.

Today I will try to keep my mouth shut and my heart open.

Do little things in an extraordinary way.
                              —PARAMAHANSA YOGANANDA

When I get too caught up in my own stuff, I do the dishes. It's a trick I learned years ago as a sweet and subtle way into meditation. Now it is a way to remind myself that all my worries are just bugs in the mind system. I really clean the dishes, and while I'm doing it, I try to remember that all I am doing is cleaning the dishes. A Vietnamese Buddhist nun once pointed out that it is a fruitless exercise. They're only going to get dirty again.

When I clean my dishes, with single-minded determination, they really get clean. They sparkle and squeak. I could sell the soap on television (if I weren't so anticorporate). Try doing your dishes until not a speck remains on any surface. Not a mote, not a dot, not one infinitesimal fleck. Then try to remember what grand problem was deviling you.

Wipe the mind dry.

It is high time the ideal of success should be replaced with the ideal of service.

—ALBERT EINSTEIN

To serve another or others is to enter fully into their lives. It is not about fixing, with the attendant assumptions of superiority. When we serve our children, we are forced to put ego and attitudes aside. Service demands humility; it demands getting dirty and feeling the suffering of another. When our children are in pain, we serve them poorly if we try to fix them. We serve them well if we tell them we know how much it hurts. And then allow ourselves to feel how much it hurts.

The children make us uncomfortable when their needs don't match our expectations. "It's time for you to grow up," we tell them, hoping they will transcend their needs when they are being needy. We speak from such a lofty place, when it is our own discomfort that needs to be transcended! The child is all right, sitting on that "pitty-pot," a very enlightened place to sit.

If I'm going to serve, I have to abandon both the High Seat and the high chair.

The destiny of the world is determined less by the battles that are lost and won than by the stories it loves and believes in.

—HAROLD GODDARD

What stories do you tell your children? My favorite story from my childhood is about a cousin, I believe, several times removed, who was captured by the Germans during the war and who escaped and survived on his own for many weeks before rejoining friendly forces. He went on to become a drifter who would occasionally drop in, unexpectedly, on the family farm in West Tennessee. Although that story is my favorite, it is only one among many. I remember only in vague sensations the storybooks, myths, and, by today's standards, primitive movies I saw. I consider myself fortunate.

Today the family stories our children are told are rarely about their own families. This is our failure as fathers. We need to tell stories to keep stories alive and we need to tell them to give life to our children. Do you really want Walt and Arnold and Steve to be your children's storytellers? Neither do I.

I can tell my family stories and enrich the future with them.

In solitude, where we are least alone.
　　　　　　　　　—LORD BYRON

The habit of ordinary solitude enriches not only the practitioner, but his family and the larger world. In solitude we are visited by spirit. Spirit is that last distinguishable entity within; the one remaining piece just outside of the inexpressible. In solitude the spirit is infused by that greater power and strenghtened. The spirit grows, the monkey mind is diminished.

Our fear of solitude is the fear of not being enough, of being haunted. It is in the realm of the hungry ghosts, our daily world, that the haunting happens. In solitude we are comforted. All that is required is the courage to go there once. Just sit. Alone. And see the face of God.

Today I can seek just ten minutes of solitude. Whom will I meet there?

A FATHER'S RESPONSIBILITY

When anyone hurts a child, it is my responsibility. When anyone heals a child, that, too, is my responsibility. How can this be?

*. . . the mystic longs for the moment when in prayer
he can, as it were, creep into God.*
— OLIVER WENDELL HOLMES, SR.

Do you pray? Think about it this way. Are there moments when you visualize an outcome, or use metaphor to describe your longing? Do you sometimes just cry out when there is no one around to hear? When you are moved by beauty or feel awe and wonder in the face of the inexpressible, do you find that you express gratitude? If yes, then you pray. If no, look more deeply.

*In prayer, we do not so much transcend the self as see it
more fully.*

The devil's name is Dullness.
—ROBERT E. LEE

My grandfather taught my father, who taught me, never to stop learning. Dad explained that to me when I was twelve and it has stayed with me. He said that it meant to always question and always seek new knowledge. He said that he knew so many men who finished their schooling and then stopped reading, stopped questioning, and, he opined, stopped living. Dull men, myopic and sated.

That ceaseless inquiry seems to lead to, at least, the doorways to wisdom and compassion. As my father lay dying, a horrible six-year process, he once whispered to me that he wouldn't wish what was happening to him on his worst enemy. I know my dad well enough to know there was no self-pity in that statement, only great understanding and compassion.

There was never anything dull about Dad. He stayed sharp by following his dad's advice. Don't stop questioning, don't stop learning.

Stay Sharp!

> *"Mean to" don't pick no cotton.*
> —ANONYMOUS

The easier way to keep all your promises is to make fewer of them. When we first start telling kids we're going to do something, play ball, take them to school, go out to dinner, read a story, always be there, they believe it absolutely. When we stop showing up for the ball game, we throw all the rest of the promises into the doubt basket. Calcium deposits form around the heart. The weight will finally break it.

It is the fathers right now, today, who need to start doing what they say they're going to do. The sorrow of the unfatherderd child is more than the planet can bear. The whole earth is weighted with the sorrow and rage of all those "mean tos." It's too damned late to mean to.

Will do, not mean to.

*If a man does not keep pace with his companions,
perhaps it is because he hears a different drummer.*
—HENRY DAVID THOREAU

This famous notion of Thoreau's has been used to excuse or justify all manner of eye-catching adult behavior, and rightly so. Our culture would be in even worse shape than it's in without the chronically out-of-step. As fathers, however, we need to listen to the drummers our children hear. The schools, mosques, churches, and other social institutions can "democratize" the soul out of a soulful child if he doesn't dance to their particular tune.

I know a kid who basically stayed in trouble his entire eighth grade year. He got detentions for cussing in class, acting up on class trips, and just generally kicking the stuffing out of quite a few stuffed shirts. I cheered him on the whole way. By the end of that year, he had gotten it all out of him, and in his freshman year became a star athlete and fine student. A class leader.

The administrators who tried to hold him down were left with dust on their hands and not one little bit of satisfaction. It was in him, and it had to come out, to paraphrase The Hook.

I'll learn to listen to the solitary drum, no matter how far away.

*In the nineteenth century inhumanity meant cruelty;
in the twentieth century it means schizoid self-
alienation.*

—ERICH FROMM

The children are immersed in a culture, which
we have created, that demands conformity to an
increasingly narrower set of standards, never self-
imposed. They live in a culture, as well, where murder on the streets is ignored, unless it's bloody
enough to compete with the nightly carnage on the
TV and where the two-dimensional gore is deplored
while the streets run with blood. They see bigotry
and horror and are told to Just Do It. Their souls
recoil at the reality of war and they run for solace
in new Outfits.

Where did they learn it? To split themselves off
from the world of nurturance to live in the world of
exploitation? How can they unlearn it? Same place.

Can we show the kids how to get Whole? How
do we start?

Put away the toys and get down on the floor.

*No one can have a higher opinion of him than I
do, and I think he's a dirty little beast.*
                                        —W. S. GILBERT

We need, we deserve, a day like this from time
to time. I don't know who Gilbert was talking about
here, but I want to. In the meantime, I'll think of
someone I can say this about, without attribution.

Enjoy your day . . .

You may call God love
you may call God goodness.
But the best name for God is compassion.
—MEISTER ECKEHART

Compassion is a fact. It is a reality, a something made visible by action. It is not a feeling. It is not pity. It is not sorrow at the wounds of the world. Compassion is the human reality of seeing the suffering of another and wishing to relieve it.

If you pray, try today to sense the word *compassion* when you say the word *God*. Get up off your knees and put legs on your prayers. If you do not pray, just for today, give it a whirl.

When you see a homeless person on the street, see him or her with God's eyes; that is, the eyes of compassion. My favorite fictional P. I., Matt Scudder, carries a pocketful of dollars and gives them to panhandlers, without judgment. Put those legs on your prayers today.

Today I will practice God.

The maturity of man—to have reacquired the seriousness he had as a child at play.
—FRIEDRICH NIETZSCHE

Watch the children at play. The seriousness with which they go at it is not grave. It is not so serious and grim that all the pleasure is ripped from it. The manner of their play is fully focused attention. Beyond the ball skittering ahead of their feet, nothing exists. The snow falling on their faces is covering the entire universe, Right Now. The sun shines everywhere. The shuttlecock spins effortlessly in space, to land, *plock,* on the racket and fly off again. The pleasure in their hearts is the true measure of their involvement in the moment at hand.

What are you waiting for? Go play!

*The silkworm weaves its cocoon and stays inside,
therefore it is imprisoned; the spider weaves its web
and stays outside, therefore it is free.*
—CHINESE PROVERB

The world comes calling. Wisdom sits just outside the gates. Sensuous involvement in self and other is just down the block. Grief, rage, and disappointment hang out on the corner. Magic and tragedy are out for a walk. In our attempts to protect the children, we deny them their birthright.

Consider this picture: The children are home, the doors are locked, the television is on. Just outside, all the riches and sorrows of the world dance on. Who is protected? Who is in prison?

Today I'll open the gates.

To stay up in the mountains is a fine thing, but the slightest attachment turns it into a market . . .
—CHINESE PROVERB

Listen to the sound the mountain makes. Can you hear the cries of the ancestors who walked it for the first time? Can you see where deadfall has become earth? Do you smell the pitch or the spring flowers? Dragonflies hover at eye level. Do you see them?

Children are not fooled by your outfit or your car or any of your pretensions.

Children become part of the mountain you become part of. That's all.

I will not reduce this great life to a marketplace.

Do not walk proudly on the earth. You cannot cleave the earth, nor can you rival the mountains in stature.

—QURAN

*H*umble and *earth* have the same Latin root, *humus*. In the fully felt presence of this great earth, we can only be humble. Be wary of those who would take your children into the mountains and forests and fail to go there filled with awe and respect. It is harmful to the child to use the earth heedlessly. We do not conquer the earth. A campground needs to become a place of respect, not a place to plunder and scar.

When I was in the Sea Scouts in Florida in the fifties, we would go to an island off the coast for long weekends. It was a wild and mysterious place to me. We didn't make bonfires, but only small fires to cook on. We left our machetes at home. One night after midnight we were swimming off a long pier and came in because the sea nettles got us. Moments later, our flashlight picked out a hammerhead shark, swimming languidly beneath the pier.

My old friend Carlton Cole, who was there that night, tells me that sacred island is now a marina and is overgrown with shops and people.

The sharks still circle.

The earth is fragile and powerful. I vow to respect it.

Look, children,
Hailstones!
Let's rush out!
—BASHŌ

We need to learn to share fully the exuberance of our children. When we are patronizing, we are not present. The poet here sees with a child's eyes the sparkling diamonds scattered on the ground and wants to **rush** out, heedless, we assume, of putting on overcoat or hat. Dance with 'em. Play on the rug, giggle, and be foolish. Open your heart and close your mind. When you enter fully into the life of your child, you are offering your blessing. When you stand back and patronize the child, you are offering only your attitude.

Today I can be fearlessly childlike!

God is a sphere whose center is everywhere and whose circumference is nowhere.
　　　　　　　　　　　　　—SAINT BONAVENTURE

Who is excluded from God's circle?

Who is excluded from yours and mine?

Whom we fear, we exclude, and our fear goes deep and often strikes close to home. Our children see whom we shun and learn to do the same. It is our opinions of others that poison our lives, and the poison spreads systemically. I recently read the yearbook of a local middle school. The inherited hatred in some of the children's profiles was painful to see.

My wife says that the one lesson she wants our children to learn is to be kind. In her way of living, she excludes no one. I try to do the same. It is not easy.

Who is excluded whom you can invite in today?

A FATHER'S RESPONSIBILITY

When my children were born, my responsibility began. It extends into the future, forever, pulled along by my father and all the fathers before him.

*In everything, do to others as you would have them
do to you . . .*

—JESUS OF NAZARETH

Unspoken in this wonderful teaching is a suggestion to stop and think deeply before acting. When
we are dealing with our children, we need to open
our own childmind in order to act lovingly and gently. When we act out of our "reactive" mind, that
child*ish* mind, we only expose attitude. Teaching is
lost.

If you mistakenly step into the street without
looking and a driver swerves to miss you and then
screams some obscenity at you, what is your reaction? It is to scream back. The driver who saved
your life has become the enemy and the cause of
your distress. If, however, she swerves and drives
on, you can look at your own dangerous preoccupa-
tion. Just so, what should you do when the child
has broken a dish?

Today I will teach as I want to learn.

Earth teach me stillness
as the grasses are stilled with light.
—FROM "EARTH TEACH ME TO REMEM-
BER"—UTE (NORTH AMERICA)

For the next several days we will try to live the couplets from this wonderful earth prayer. Our greatest teacher surrounds us at all times, and we miss her teachings completely. As fathers, we must return to consciousness of this great earth and, through our example, lead our children to her as well.

When the grasses are stilled with the light, they are not oblivious. They are, rather, fully alive. Just so, as we practice stillness, we find our minds focusing to a fine point, our hearts beating strongly and steadily, and our senses fully alert to the present moment. Can you see a field of grasses, brilliant and alive in the sunlight? Can you for a moment today *be* that field of grass?

Today I vow to ask the earth to teach me stillness.

Earth teach me suffering
as old stones suffer with memory.

Today, if possible, find a stone and spend some time sitting with it. This is a daring exercise. Please be daring. Sit with your stone and allow yourself to imagine what has brought it to you. What can you read of glacial shift or thermal heat in its surface?

We must learn not to turn away from suffering. Compassion is a fact of life, and our lives are diminished if we do not allow it full exposure. As you sit with your stone and ask for its teaching, listen closely. You will meet your compassion.

Today I vow to ask the earth to teach me suffering.

Earth teach me humility
as blossoms are humble with beginning.

The idea of humility has a hard time of it. It is often confused with humiliation or the bugaboo of low self-esteem. Twelve-steppers talk of the fear of becoming the "hole in the doughnut." (Not so. Without the hole, no doughnut.) Humility comes from *humus,* which gives us earth as well. To become humble is to become, in a sense, earthy, thus interdependent.

Spring blossoms are not timid; they simply are rich with promise and totally codependent. They arise codependently with sun and rain and rich earth. (Without the blossom, humble in its beginning, no flower.)

Humility comes from recognizing our place in the fabric of things. No more, no less.

Today I vow to ask the earth to teach me humility.

Earth teach me caring
as the mother who secures her young.

The mother cares for her child with no thought of separation. When the mother feeds her child, she is totally present. When she heals the child, she is feeling the pain. When she plays with her child, she is all play, with the ever-present watcher, alert to danger. The mother caring for her child is fully absorbed in her task.

I grew up on a farm, part-time, and would go to the barn early in the morning to watch the animals begin their day. Sows, mares, and cows would be with their young. There were barn cats as well, wild and wily, nestled in the hayloft nursing kittens. I was too young to romanticize what I saw. It wasn't cute. It was enrapturing. Such care is so difficult today. We are blessed to be surrounded by teachers of caring.

Today I vow to ask the earth to teach me caring.

Earth teach me courage
as the tree which stands all alone.

In our deepest selves, if we listen closely, we will know the truth and the way in every situation. Courage comes in looking deeply and then acting in congruence with that deep knowing. If we turn away from looking deeply or if we refuse to act on what we have seen in moments of spiritual candor, we are denying ourselves the reality of courage.

Primary courage then is simply the courage to look. This looking is done with openness, free of opinions, and with willingness to be challenged, and with the honesty of true inquiry. And it is done by asking for help. This is not the courage of the monk on his cushion, it is the courage of a free person, in the world of comings and goings. The solitary tree, after all, is not so solitary. It draws its courage from the totality of its environment, including is deep-rootedness.

Today I vow to ask the earth to teach me courage.

Earth teach me limitation
as the ant which crawls on the ground.

We are imperfect and limited. Both Bruno Bettelheim and D. W. Winnicott talk of the "good enough" parent. It is only when we accept our limitations as parents that we are able to be effective at all. Otherwise we murder our abilities with our incessant quest for perfection.

I have the patience to teach my kids to cook, to swim, to ride bikes, and to walk respectfully in the mountains. I do not have the patience to get them to clean their rooms or do their laundry. So I don't try. Their rooms are OK, and when they run out of clothes, they clean them, after a day of being stinky and unkempt.

Today I vow to ask the earth to teach me my limitations.

Earth teach me freedom
as the eagle which soars in the sky.

The spirited father learns that true freedom is something other than what he expected. It is not the freedom of economic security or the freedom to behave childishly and dress it up as freedom of expression. It is rather the paradoxical freedom of choosing what you have. It is the freedom to act courageously and humbly according to a freely articulated code, based on sure moral and ethical principles, individual to himself. True freedom is to be free from the prison of the mind.

The children can see the chains that bind us. When he was only three, Willie saw that I was sad one day and told me that I needed to cry. I was trapped in the macho prison of not letting my children see me cry. John said to me one day, when I was trapped in my get-a-Porsche mania, "Imagine how stupid you'd feel if you woke up one day to find you'd actually bought one." Trapped again in the external miasma. A friend's daughter, at age two, opened the refrigerator and, seeing all the beer, said, "Daddy." He stopped drinking a week later. Listen to the kids. They see your prison bars.

Today I vow to ask the earth to teach me freedom.

Earth teach me resignation
as the leaves which die in the fall.

There is a wonderful story of the Buddhist master who, when asked what his teachings were, responded by holding up a glass and saying, "I see this glass as already broken." He went on to say that although the glass was whole and he enjoyed very much drinking his delicious tea from it, he knew that someday it would fall from the table and be shattered. How much more precious the glass was, when he knew that it was already broken. That story touched me deeply. I try to see my children and those I love as already broken. When I do, my heart blossoms. This is not a maudlin exercise, although it could easily become one. Be careful.

Today I vow to ask the earth to teach me resignation.

Earth teach me regeneration
as the seed which rises in the spring.

We can begin anew at any moment. Letting go of past mistakes or recent errors is the practice of regeneration. The body, mind, and spirit can be renewed in simple ways. There is nothing to fear in starting over or in starting something entirely new. We are reborn in every moment.

If you have been angry with a child, say that you're sorry. Don't just "make nice" and pretend it never happened. It happened and the child will not forget. When the conscious father admits his fault, hope and love are regenerated.

When you are unhappy with your work, consider deeply the source of your unhappiness. Do so without fixing blame, especially being careful not to blame yourself. What can be reborn? Take solace in the knowledge of eternal spring.

Today I vow to ask the earth to teach me regeneration.

Earth teach me to forget myself
as melted snow forgets its life.

Can you see this "self" as already broken? What I call "myself" is mutating and impermanent. When I form some rigid idea of self, I begin to cause trouble. The whine of the injured "me" consumes my family and my friends. I need to constantly return to the center of my life and see how, without those friends and that family, there would be no "me."

I am most useful and most at peace when I put aside my self-centered concerns, when I stop defending this illusory "self" and enter fully into life. Saint Francis said, "It is in self-forgetting that I am found." Zen master Dogen said, "To study the self is to forget the self. The forget the self is to be enlightened by the ten thousand things."

Today I vow to ask the earth to teach me self-forgetting.

Earth teach me to remember kindness
as the dry fields weep with rain.

Just be kind. That is a core teaching of so many grand philosophies and religions. Our best stories are stories of kindness. Our best moments, if we look deeply, are when we step out of the circle of self and into the life of other.

If we want our children to live in the world of nurturance rather than the world of exploitation, then we need to teach them kindness, and the only way to teach it is to be it. It is so difficult. We struggle to protect our ideas and we sacrifice our hearts. We set up a world of us and them, self and other, right and wrong, black and white, and are caught in a dismaying and spiritless snare, hobbled and twisting in smaller and smaller circles. Simple kindness frees us.

What can you do to teach kindness?

Today I vow to ask the earth to teach me kindness.

You do live longer with bran, but you spend the last fifteen years on the toilet.

—ALAN KING

How serious are you about your health? You know what to eat. Lighten up.

Don't expect any more here. This fathering business is a gracious dance, full of magic and tragedy. And a dash of dopey fun. Take it too seriously and bran will be the best your diet will ever get.

Lighten up.

Now, don't get upset, we tell the kids when what we should be saying is Get Upset. Get good and upset and go off somewhere where no one is going to tell you how to feel, how you should feel, or what to do to get over how you feel. If you need to go somewhere, we need to say, and exercise all those elaborate multisyllabic words you giggle about at school, then please do so. Let it rip.

Who are we to say watch your mouth?

Why, in fact, should we watch our mouths? There are times when we need to behave like mountain gorillas. The trick for us, the grown-ups, is to watch ourselves doing it. Just step back and notice how closely we resemble an old silverback in high temper.

There is a place for contained malediction.

It is only through the mystery of self-sacrifice that man may find himself anew.
—CARL GUSTAV JUNG

What is the mountain you are willing to die on? The senseless preservation of self does great harm to the father and to the children. The endless sacrifice of the self ennobles the children because it provides them the space to grow. I said to Willie once, inhabited by the spirit of Mr. Rogers, that he didn't need to act silly—that we love him just the way he is. He informed me, without missing a beat, that silly *is* the way he is. I had missed that because my self-centered ideas of how he should be got in the way. A father's mountain rears in the kitchen.

The resurrection is a daily reality when we get out of our own ways.

*Whoever teaches his son teaches not only his son
but also his son's son—and so on to the end of
generations.*

—THE TALMUD

The reality of this simple idea is repeated
throughout the world's religions and their meeker
cousins, psychologies and philosophies.

My great-grandfather is present in my life today
as sure as if he had just walked in from the cornfields
out back of the family home in rural Mississippi.
My great-grandchild will bear the imprint of my life
just as certainly as I carry distant Bill McLeod.

Contemplate this carefully. Fathers need to consider the effect of their lives today on generations
they will never see.

My actions today are for my great-great-grandchild.

> *. . . everything matters.*
> —BLAISE PASCAL

There is no inconsequential act. Our lives are made up of every action we have ever taken. The ripple from a harsh judgment made in a drunken moment can create a tidal wave of sadness. Just so, a kind word spoken in the darkness can bring light a thousand years later.

When fathers consider the effect of every action they take involving the little ones near them, prudence and simplicity can be actualized. It is no small thing to be a father. It matters very much.

Being a father has consequences.

Every blade of grass has its Angel that bends over it and whispers, "Grow, grow."

—THE TALMUD

This is a good day to remember that you are not in charge. The children are growing with the help and the love of the entire universe. Be careful not to get in the way.

Growing, growing.

All shall be well, and all shall be well and all manner of things shall be well.
—JULIAN OF NORWICH

At a time of intense personal turmoil, no work and no hope for work, being evicted from my apartment, living in a strange city with few friends, and riddled with guilt over a past I could no longer deny, I turned to an Episcopal church for solace. I walked in and said I needed to talk with a priest. Within minutes I was sitting in a comfortable office, sunlit on this fall day, and was unburdening myself. Fear after fear after fear poured out of me, and this gentle priest listened with great love. We were together for over an hour, and that hour marked my return to a religious life.

Months later, in a confirmation class in that same church, I heard these words of Julian of Norwich for the first time. Certainly it was the timing, and certainly it was that I read a version of them in T. S. Eliot and certainly it was my openness that caused them to strike me so deeply; but it is certain as well that it is the rhythm and the truth of these words that have caused them to endure and to touch so many of us.

Today take the words of this great mystic into your heart.

Ye shall know the truth and the truth shall make you mad.
—ALDOUS HUXLEY

Hey, have a nice day!

Our pure mind is in the depraved one.
　　　　　　　　　　　　—HUI NENG

There is not some other that either possesses us or will cure us. It's all in there. When I am angry, for example, I need to understand that anger is not a thing visited on me from somewhere else. It is what I am and it can end. Anger is transformed by and to wisdom. When I am feeling hopeless, I can understand that hope resides in the same place as hopelessness. When I am feeling lack, I can understand abundance. They coexist. Right here and now.

As a father, I need to work on watering the seeds I need to father. When I most want to run away, I must stay still. When I am most afraid, I must act with courage. When I feel my child's sorrow, I must know her joy. None of these seeds are someplace else. I contain them all.

I'll look at both sides of the page today.

The true teacher defends his pupils against his own personal influence.

—BRONSON ALCOTT

We live in a time when there are teachers and pundits who are so taken with their own charisma and learning that they forget their obligation to just shut up from time to time. When you meet such a person, run. If your children are in the company of such a person, carry them away.

If you are such a person, then look more deeply for the wise teacher you carry within you. Our generations of pedagogy have gotten us into trouble for too long. One of a father's hardest tasks is to teach with the absolute willingness to let the teaching be obliterated by the experience and good common sense of the child.

The kids deserve some room to make their own mistakes.

Rings and jewels are not gifts but apologies for gifts.
The only true gift is a portion of thyself.
                    —RALPH WALDO EMERSON

We guard that part of ourselves we most need to set free. So many fathers will give the kids anything they want, within their abilities to do so, and will deny the children the one thing they most need—a little piece of their heart. The heart expands to fill the room where it's needed. When we give it away, it grows; when we guard it, it atrophies.

Giving a little piece of the heart can mean feeling the suffering of the child. It can mean facing the reality that this person is not you. It can mean seeing that this person is not what you would have him to be. Giving up a little piece of the heart can mean disappointment and sorrow. We don't want to risk that and our hearts harden. The suffering of the unfathered child continues relentlessly.

My heart grows as I give pieces away.

To the man who is afraid, everything rustles.
                                        —SOPHOCLES

We can say, "Other parents are lying to get special privileges for their kids. That's scary, so I'm
going to do it too." Or we can say, "I'm afraid I'm
not doing enough for my child." Look at the relief
in that second one. The moment we name the fear,
it takes on a smaller mien. Few of us really feel, if
we look closely enough, that we are not doing
enough. But when we place the source of our fears
elsewhere than in ourselves, we live surrounded by
threats.

We build walls to keep the world out and we
succeed. The world never gets in to bless our children with its richness and its delicate warp and
woof. In walling the world out, we establish a petri
dish for our fears. In the stockade, our lives are
bland. Outside, all is banal.

We overcome our fears by owning them. "That
scares me" is irresponsible. "I'm afraid" is the beginning of the end of fear.

Tear down the walls.

Fear not that your life shall come to an end, but rather that it shall never have a beginning.
—JOHN HENRY NEWMAN

The poet reminds us that he not busy being born is busy dying. My father taught me never to stop learning. Both, I believe, are saying that we can wake up or we can spend our lives entranced. Look closely at the day ahead. What plans are you making, what ideas are perking away, what do you fear, what do you anticipate?

Where is the room for a surprise? What if today is the day to begin your life?

It is.

> *It is easier for a father to have children than for children to have a real father.*
>
> —POPE JOHN XXIII

What does a *real* father do? How is a real father different from some other, presumably not real, father?

When he is there, he is there, not elsewhere.

He does not turn over the task of fathering, even the smallest details, to someone else.

He knows the value of the gift he has been given.

He suffers.

What else?

Sell your cleverness and buy bewilderment.
                                           —RUMI

Today we can try to look around us without knowing what we are seeing. Even when we know what we are seeing, we can dismiss the knowledge and look with fresh eyes at what shows up. We can look with a child's eyes and live for a while in awe and wonder rather than in cynical understanding.

Today I will live bewildered.

When a father complains that his son has taken to evil ways, what should he do? Love him more than ever.

—BA'AL SHEM TOV

The love we show to a troubling child will nurture him in the ways of love while the disapproval will only stunt him. One way to love such a child is to use just the word used in that first sentence. *Troubling*, not *troubled* or *in trouble*.

When we say that the child we love is troubling, we are telling the truth, about ourselves, and freeing ourselves to love the child. The trouble becomes personal and we become responsible for helping—there is a conspiracy to see the end of trouble.

The father and the child determine that what must win is their relationship.

The child and the father fight the trouble, not each other.

O God, make us children of quietness, and heirs of peace.

—SAINT CLEMENT

It's so noisy. It's so warlike. Can we begin to see that if we pray for quiet, the answer is in our becoming quiet? Can we begin to understand that when we pray for peace, the answer is in our developing a peaceful heart?

This is a grave business. In a time of so much noise and so little peace, our children suffer and we fail to hear the suffering over the tumult. Can we bring quiet into our hearts and then let it radiate into our homes? Can we bring peace into our hearts and let that spread as well? To end the suffering of the children, or at least to hear it?

Shhh.

The secret of life is balance, and the absence of balance is life's destruction.
—HAXRAT INAYAT KHAN

Body, mind, and spirit in wholesome balance is the ideal. When we are able to actively practice the spiritual, the other two come along. I cannot be useful to my children when I am physically off—Bill in a carbohydrate stupor does not have a mind alert to nuance, and the spirit is head-down in the chocolate cake. Bill off in his head figuring it all out loses intuition and spontaneity, and overeats in the bargain. Bill stuck off in his meditation room or carrying around his koan when the children need to go pick the corn is suffering from a glut of spiritual materialism.

Lighten up—balance comes easy.

Do not weep; do not wax indignant. Understand.
　　　　　　　　　—BENEDICT DE SPINOZA

There is no love without understanding. When our children "fail" us, it is our lack of understanding that makes it so. When they "do not live up to their potential," it is our failure to understand their potential that makes it so. For every moment that our own desires, prejudices, and delusions rule our vision of our children, for just that long are they not fully loved.

Today I will seek to understand.

Don't limit a child to your own learning, for he was born in another time.
—AUTHOR UNKNOWN

There is an abyss of time between father and child that the father cannot cross and the child must not cross. My knowledge of being fourteen and my son's knowledge of being fourteen are tempered by different mores, different cultures, and different, so very different, times. The urgings are the same. The needs are the same. It is the knowing that is different. The gulf can never be crossed, but love will temper the hurt and provide the net when he falls. What I must know is that I cannot stop him from falling in the first place without injuring him more deeply than the fall ever will.

I will celebrate the difference between me and my children. I will keep the net spread.

*Out beyond ideas of wrongdoing and rightdoing,
there is a field. I'll meet you there.*

—RUMI

The spirited father can meet his children in a place where there is no judgment. Freed from the need to criticize or praise, he can sit down on the floor and open his being to the children until he disappears.

You have had that feeling in your life. It can be created, with practice, at any moment. That practice is to let go of the chattering judgmental mind. Just shake your head or twitch your nose. Then sit down on the floor. Let the kids in. They'll disappear as well.

I will practice self-forgetting.

Bees are not as busy as we think they are. They just can't buzz any slower.

—KEN HUBBARD

Just for the merry hell of it, question some general assumption today. Make it your sole business as you go about all the rest of your business to puncture some balloon or another. How about "The candidates really like each other." Or "It's not the money."

Lighten up. Ask irreverent questions.

During the first period of a man's life the greatest danger is: not to take the risk.
—SØREN KIERKEGAARD

When we overprepare the children for that period just after leaving home, we are taking the risk of twisting their feet on the path they were destined to take. They will get back to that path, probably, but not without more pain and horror than might have been necessary. If we say, "I want my daughter to be a lawyer," we are missing the mark. We must say that we want her to be herself. We do not know ahead of time what risks the children are going to need to take. They don't, after all. You can't prepare a future ballerina for the rigors of toe shoes when she wants to be a veterinarian with all of her eleven-year-old heart.

We must not deny the ones we love the chance to fail or the chance to blaze like a meteor in service to our fears. We can tell them of the risks we have taken, but we cannot tell them which ones to take or which ones to avoid.

I can encourage the child to invest total body, mind, and spirit in what I may think is folly. I will keep the net spread.

A child becomes an adult when he realizes he has a right not only to be right but also to be wrong.
—THOMAS SZASZ

We can offer our children wisdom or we can offer them our attitude. We can offer our love or we can offer our opinion. We can show them our imperfections or we can lie about our lives.

We can offer them a life in the world of nurturance or in the world of exploitation.

Most likely, we'll do all these things. The trick is to watch ourselves and treat ourselves and our children with the three qualities of Lao-tze: simplicity, compassion, and patience.

I can be a "good enough" father.

What is within us is also without
What is without us is also within.

—THE UPANISHADS

APPENDIX A

A Day of Mindfulness

This is a simple practice with profound long-term effects. It is born from the earliest teachings of the historical Buddha and was given new life by Zen Master Thich Nhat Hanh and the members of his Tiep Hien order during the days of the Vietnam War. Its intent then and for you today is to provide a time of self-care and renewal. I commend any of Thich Nhat Hanh's books to you for a deeper understanding of the value of mindfulness than I would ever be able to teach.

The core of a Day of Mindfulness is full awareness of the present moment. If you can do this, to even the smallest degree on just this day, right now, then you will be beginning a powerful spiritual practice, not connected to any sect or dogma. In my practice I choose the days in advance. What I am asking you to do is more difficult. I am asking you, without advance warning, to radically change the way you go about your day.

Here is how it works:

> Spend this day alone to the degree that you are able to do so.
>
> Spend this day in silence, again, to the degree that you can.

Do not read the newspaper or magazines today.

Turn off the TV, radio, stereo, and leave them off.

Cook your own meals today. Shop for the ingredients for each meal and pay attention to the cooking.

When you eat your meals, taste the food. Consider how this food came to you. Consider who brought it to you and how it was farmed.

Do not be a consumer today. Buy nothing that is not absolutely essential to your life.

Take at least one long walk today. As you walk, breathe in and out consciously and remind yourself that with each step you are returning to your true home.

In the evening, read poetry or spiritual literature. If there is a type of music that soothes you, listen to it. Better yet, make music of your own.

Whenever you find yourself getting upset or discover that you have lost your way, stop and breathe. Breathe in and out, three times, slowly, and say to yourself that you know you are breathing in and breathing out.

At bedtime, stay awake for a while. Look gently back over your day. Do so without judging or comment. Simply let the day be finished.